CONSUMERGUIDE®

PLANT IT, GROW IT, ENJOY IT

Betty Barr Mackey

Susan McClure, M.S.

C. Colston Burrell, M.S., Consultant

Publications International, Ltd.

3 1336 07489 1293

Betty Barr Mackey is a garden writer, lecturer, and publisher. She is a coauthor of *The Gardener's Home Companion, Cutting Gardens,* and *Carefree Plants.* Her publishing company, B. B. Mackey Books, covers specialized horticultural subjects. She is a member of the North American Rock Garden Society and the Garden Writers Association.

Susan McClure, M.S., author of more than a dozen gardening books including *The Herb Gardener* and *Culinary Gardens from Design to Palate,* taught at the Chicago Botanic Garden and Morton Arboretum and was formerly a regional director of the Garden Writers of America.

C. Colston Burrell, M.S. (consultant), is a Master of Landscape Architecture and has an M.S. in horticulture. He is a garden designer, writer, consultant, and photographer, and is president of Native Landscape Design and Restoration, Ltd. He coauthored the *Illustrated Encyclopedia of Perennials,* contributed to the *New Encyclopedia of Organic Gardening and Landscaping with Nature,* and has served as consultant to many gardening books, including *Treasury of Gardening.*

Contributing writer: **Wayne Ambler, M.S.**

Picture credits:
Front cover: **Derek Fell** (top center, bottom center & bottom right); **Jerry Pavia** (top left & bottom left); **Natural Visions** (top right).
Back cover: **Derek Fell** (top & bottom); **PIL Collection** (center).

Artville: 188; **Brand X Pictures:** 24; **Gay Bumgarner:** 75, 77; **Crandall & Crandall:** 72; McIntire, 285; **Digital Vision:** 193; **Derek Fell:** 8, 10, 14, 31, 34, 39, 53, 55, 58, 59, 62, 69, 71, 88, 97 (top), 134, 154, 156, 160, 167, 173, 191, 194, 204, 212, 220, 231, 259 (top), 276, 292; **Pamela Harper:** 123, 124, 126, 157 (bottom), 289; **Betty Barr Mackey:** 18; **George & Judy Manna:** 70 (top); **Natural Visions:** 38, 40, 49, 60 (bottom), 150, 162, 175, 182, 208, 233, 269, 290, 298; **Jerry Pavia:** 30, 32, 67, 96, 107 (bottom), 116, 117, 119, 127 (bottom), 130, 133, 136, 137, 139, 148, 149, 161, 165, 178, 181, 189, 190, 196, 197, 222, 224, 226, 232, 237, 239 (bottom), 245, 253, 255, 256, 258, 262, 268, 286, 288; **Ben Phillips:** 85 (bottom); **PhotoDisc:** 17, 21, 27, 44, 68, 81, 85 (top), 99, 115, 151, 168, 169, 172, 177, 179, 186, 192, 195, 200, 203, 209, 214, 215, 216, 223, 246, 261, 266, 279, 282, 293; **PIL Collection:** 5, 6, 13, 105, 143; **Positive Images:** Patricia J. Bruno, 51, 98, 271; Gay Bumgarner, 131, 141, 257; Karen Bussolini, 272; Margaret Hensel, 118; Jerry Howard, 11, 248, 249, 270, 294; Jim Kahnwiler, 218; Pam Spaulding, 273; **Ann Reilly:** 265; **Richard Shiell:** 52, 170, 241, 252, 260, 291, 297 (bottom); **Carol Simowitz:** 128, 145, 152, 228 (bottom); **SuperStock:** 65, 281, 301.

Contributing Illustrators: **Taylor Bruce, Marlene Hill Donnelly, Joyce Shelton, Jody Wheeler**

Louis Weber, CEO
Publications International, Ltd.
7373 North Cicero Avenue
Lincolnwood, Illinois 60712

Permission is never granted for commercial purposes.

Manufactured in China.

8 7 6 5 4 3 2 1

ISBN: 1-4127-1248-3

CONTENTS

Creating a Garden

Have you always dreamed of starting a garden of your own but were never quite sure where to begin? Or perhaps you are interested in improving your existing landscape but need a few helpful hints? Whether you're a gardening novice or a seasoned pro, *Plant It, Grow It, Enjoy It* contains the practical advice you'll need to minimize your effort and maximize your results.

This book begins with the basics. By focusing just a little extra attention on fundamental things like soil, water, and light, you can make a major difference in your garden. Perhaps you need to do a soil test to determine if you should adjust the nutrients in the dirt, or maybe you need to switch the time of day that you're watering your plants. Any extra time and effort you spend in the

garden early on will ensure an even greater reward at bloom or harvest time. We'll also discuss how to prevent pests and diseases from ruining your handiwork, how you can propagate your plants to increase your own supply or share with a friend, and how organic and low-maintenance gardening can add to the ease and enjoyment of this popular hobby.

Once you've covered the fundamentals, you can begin to outline your landscape plans. With a seemingly limit-less choice of annuals, perennials, and woody plants, you can tailor your design to fit your individual needs. Each part of the landscape is important, and we'll help you decide how to make the most of your garden. We'll also give you hints about bulbs, roses, ground covers, and vines. With a little planning and our helpful hints you can create a landscape filled with an abundance of flowers, trees, and greenery. Dig in!

Gardening Basics

To succeed in cultivation, most plants need good soil with suitable drainage and texture. They need moisture and light to keep them healthy and thriving. These basics provide an important foundation for any yard or garden, and with our helpful hints, you'll be sure to get off to a good start. The tips included here will help you enhance your landscape—and maybe even your enjoyment of gardening.

THE DIRT ON SOIL

Good soil is the first step to a great garden. The loose, dark earth of the fabulous gardens seen on television and in magazines doesn't usually just happen. It is created by gardeners improving their native soils. Soils can be amended with sand to make them looser and drier or with clay to make them moister and firmer. They can be given plentiful doses of organic material—old leaves, ground-up twigs, rotted livestock manure, and old lawn clippings to improve texture and structure. Organic matter nourishes any kind of soil, which, in turn, encourages better plant growth.

START WITH THE RIGHT PLANTS

Use plants adapted to the conditions right outside your door. When plants prefer your native soil and climate, no matter how difficult these conditions may be, they are more likely to grow beautifully with little effort. Native plants—shade trees, shrubs, or flowers that arise in the nearby countryside—are good options. Or, try less common plants from faraway places with conditions similar to your own.

■ To identify suitable plants, begin by identifying your garden conditions. Have your soil tested or do your own tests (see pages 11–20) to determine if you have a light and sandy soil, a moderate and productive soil, or a heavy clay soil.

■ Watch the site to see how sunny it is, and select plants that need full sun, partial sun, or shade, accordingly.

Make sure your soil has been thoroughly prepared before you start to plant.

■ Find your location on the United States Department of Agriculture hardiness zone map (see pages 312–313), which indicates average minimum winter temperature.

■ Make a note of the light levels, soil conditions, and climatic zone information you've found. Then check nursery catalogs and gardening books to find plants that thrive in every one of the elements particular to your yard. Use these plants as a shopping list for all your future gardening projects. A little extra legwork in the beginning makes gardening much easier over the coming years.

■ Look for the tales weeds have to tell as they grow in your garden. Weeds are opportunists, taking advantage of any vacant soil to make their home. (Just think of how well this strategy has benefited the dandelion, a native of Eurasia that has swept through America.)

Although they seem to grow everywhere, dandelions prefer fertile, often heavy soil. Likewise, other weeds favor certain kinds of soil. For instance, acidic soil can encourage the growth of

These unwanted plantains are a sign that the soil may be acidic.

crabgrass, plantains, sheep sorrel, and horsetails. Alkaline soil (also called sweet or basic soil) is favored by chamomile and goosefoot. Fertile, near-neutral soils can provide a nurturing environment for redroot pigweed, chickweed, dandelions, and wild mustard.

■ Even if you can't tell one weed from another, you can find out important infor-mation by looking at them closely. If a vacant garden area has few weeds taking advantage of the opening, the soil is likely to need plenty of work. If weeds are growing, but only sparsely, and have short, stunted stems and discolored leaves, the area may have a nutrient deficiency, and a soil test is in order. If, in newly tilled soil, weeds sprout up quickly in certain areas and more slowly in others, the weedy areas are likely to be moister and better for seed germination.

■ Grow a plant for at least two or three years before you decide to remove it. It can take that long for a perennial plant to get comfortable in a new home and begin to really show what it can do. Allowing a trial period of several years also lets the plant get beyond setbacks from difficult weather— slow growth after an exceptionally cold winter or poor flowering during a long drought, for instance.

■ Don't assume you can't grow a plant if it dies once. If you like that plant

and are willing to buy another one, put it in a different place—one better suited for its light and soil needs.

SOIL TESTING

Get a soil test before you start adding fertilizers and amendments to your garden soil. This follows the old advice, "If it ain't broke, don't fix it." Some-

A soil test will tell you which of these soil amendments are needed—or whether your soil even needs amending at all.

SOME SOURCES OF SPECIFIC NUTRIENTS

Many of these fertilizers are available processed and packaged.

Nitrogen: livestock manure (composted), bat guano, chicken manure, fish emulsion, blood meal, kelp meal, cottonseed meal

Phosphorus: bonemeal, rock phosphate, super phosphate

Potassium: granite meal, sulfate of potash, green-sand, wood ashes, seabird guano, shrimp shell meal

Calcium: bonemeal, limestone, eggshells, wood ashes, oyster shells, chelated calcium

Boron: manure, borax, chelated boron

Copper: chelated copper

Magnesium: Epsom salts, dolomitic limestone, chelated magnesium

Sulfur: sulfur, solubor, iron sulfate, zinc sulfate

Zinc: zinc sulfate, chelated zinc

Iron: chelated iron, iron sulfate

times unnecessary tampering with nutrients or soil acidity can actually create more problems than benefits.

■ Soil tests tell you the nutrient levels in your soil, a plant version of the nutrient guides on packaged foods. They also note pH and organic content, two factors important to overall smooth sailing from the ground up.

■ To have your soil tested, call your local Cooperative Extension Service, often listed under state or county government in the phone book. Ask them how to get a soil-testing kit, which contains a soil-collecting bag and instructions. Follow the directions precisely for accurate results. The results may come as a chart full of numbers, which can be a little intimidating at first. But if

Pay attention to soil conditions now, and you'll be rewarded with a healthy, beautiful garden later.

you look carefully for the following, you can begin to interpret these numbers:

- If the percentage of organic matter is under 5 percent, the garden needs some extra compost.

- Nutrients will be listed separately, possibly in parts per million. Sometimes they are also rated as available in high, medium, or low levels. If an element or two comes in on the low side, you'll want to add a fertilizer that replaces what's lacking.

- Soil pH refers to the acidity of the soil. Ratings below 7 are acidic soils. From 6 to

Ground limestone, used to raise the pH level of acidic soil, should be spread evenly and then tilled into the soil.

7 are slightly acidic, the most fertile pH range. Above 7 is alkaline or basic soil, which can become problematic above pH 8. Excessively acidic and alkaline soils can be treated to make them more moderate and productive.

- Add only the nutrients your soil test says are necessary. More is not always better when it comes to plant nutrients. Don't feel compelled to add a little bit more of a fertilizer that promises great results. Too much of any one nutrient can actually produce toxic results, akin to disease or worse. Buy and apply only what's required, and save the rest of your money for a better use, like more plants.

PH LEVELS

It is always best to choose plants that thrive in the pH of your existing soil. If you must alter the pH, follow the guidelines below.

- Use ground limestone to raise the pH of acidic soils. Limestone is nature's soil sweetener, capable of neutralizing overly acidic soils. It's best to add limestone in the fall to allow time for it to begin to dissolve and do its job. The amount of limestone pine needles. These soil amendments gradually acidify the soil while improving its texture. Garden sulfur is a reliable cure when added as recommended in a soil test. It acidifies the soil slowly as microbes convert the sulfur to sulfuric acid and other compounds.

■ Maintaining the new and improved pH is an ongoing project. Recheck the soil's pH every year and continue to add amendments as needed.

TEXTURE CHECKUP

Check the texture of your soil in a jar filled with water. This test is simple to do at home and provides important information about your soil.

■ Gather some soil from the garden, choosing a sample from near the surface and

you use will vary depending on the specific soil conditions. Simple home test kits, or a professional test, can be used to determine the soil's pH. If you dump limestone on soil randomly, you run the risk of overdosing the soil. Follow guidelines on the limestone package or on a soil test.

■ To lower the alkalinity and increase the fertility of limey and other soils with very high pH, add cottonseed meal, sulfur, pine bark, compost, or down to a depth of 8 inches. If you have dry clay, pulverize it into fine granules, and mix well. Put a 1-inch layer (a little over a cup) in a quart glass jar with ¼ teaspoon powdered dishwasher detergent. (Dishwasher detergent won't foam up.) Add enough water to fill the jar ⅔ full. Shake the jar for a minute, turning it upside down as needed to get all the soil off the bottom, then put the jar on a counter where it can sit undisturbed.

■ One minute later, mark the level of settled particles on the jar with a crayon or wax pencil. This is sand. Five minutes later, mark the

Knowing the texture of your soil can help you determine which plants will grow well in your garden and how much care they will need.

If your soil has equal percentages of sand, silt, and clay, you probably won't need to amend it.

amount of silt that has settled out. Over the next hour or so, the clay will slowly settle out and allow you to take the final measurement. These measurements show the relative percentages of sand, silt, and clay—the texture of your soil.

• Soil that has a high percentage of sand (70 percent or more) tends to be well aerated, ready to plant earlier in spring. But it also tends to need more frequent watering and fertilization than heavier soils.

• Soil that has 35 percent or more clay retains moisture well, so it takes longer to dry in spring and may need less watering in summer. It can be richer and is more likely to produce lush growth with just the addition of compost and, occasionally, a little fertilizer. The compost is important. It helps break up clay so the soil won't be too dense and poorly aerated.

• Soil that has nearly equal percentages of sand, silt,

and clay can have intermediate characteristics and is generally well suited for good gardening.

TESTING DRAINAGE

Test your soil's drainage by digging a hole, filling it with water, and watching how quickly the water disappears. All the soil tests in the world won't do a better job than this simple project. It tells you how quickly moisture moves through the soil and whether the soil is likely to be excessively dry or very soggy—neither of which is ideal.

■ When it hasn't rained for a week or more and the soil is dry, dig several holes that are 1 foot deep and 2 feet wide. Fill them to the top with water and keep track of how long it takes for the holes to empty. Compare your findings to the following scale:

- 1 to 12 minutes: The soil is sharply drained and likely to be dry.

- 12 to 30 minutes: The soil has ideal drainage.

- 30 minutes to 4 hours: Drainage is slow but adequate for plants that thrive in moist soil.

- Over 4 hours: Drainage is poor and needs help.

SOIL AMENDMENTS

Once you know the nature of your soil, it's easy to amend it to meet the needs of the plants you want to grow.

■ Add a thick layer of mulch and let it rot to improve the soil of existing gardens. Minerals, released as the mulch is degraded into nutrient soup, soak down into the soil and fertilize existing plants. Humic acid, another product of decay, clumps together small particles of clay to make a lighter soil. For best success, remember these points:

- Woody mulch, such as shredded bark, uses nitrogen as it decays. Apply extra nitrogen to prevent the decay process from consuming soil nitrogen that plants need for growth.

- Don't apply fine-textured mulches, like grass clippings, in thick layers that can mat down and smother the soil.

Designated paths, such as this stone walkway, allow you to move through the garden without compacting the soil and planting beds.

• Use mulch, which helps keep the soil moist, in well-drained areas that won't become soggy or turn into breeding grounds for plant-eating slugs and snails.

■ Get local compost from your city or town hall service department. Made from leaves and grass clippings collected as a public service, the compost may be free or at least reasonably priced for local residents. To find other

SOURCES OF ORGANIC MATTER

Compost

Livestock manure

Straw

Grass clippings

Salt hay

Shredded bark

Bark chunks

Shredded leaves

Seedless weeds

Peat moss

Kitchen vegetable scraps

Mushroom compost

Agricultural remains, such
   as peanut hulls, rice hulls,
   or ground corncobs

large-scale composters, check with the nearest Cooperative Extension Service; they are up-to-date on these matters. Or try landscapers and nurseries, who may compost fall leaves or stable leftovers for their customers; and bulk soil dealers, who may sell straight compost or premium topsoil blended with compost. Don't give up. Yard scraps are discouraged or banned in many American landfills, so someone near you may be composting them.

■ Plan ahead for bulky organic soil amendments—compost, manure, and leaves—that may be added by the wheelbarrow-load to improve the soil. This will raise the soil level, at least temporarily. As the organic matter decays, the soil level will lower.

• If soils rich in organic matter drop to expose the top of a newly planted shrub or tree roots, add

more soil or organic matter to keep the roots under cover.

• If your garden is beside a house or fence, keep the soil level low enough so it won't come in contact

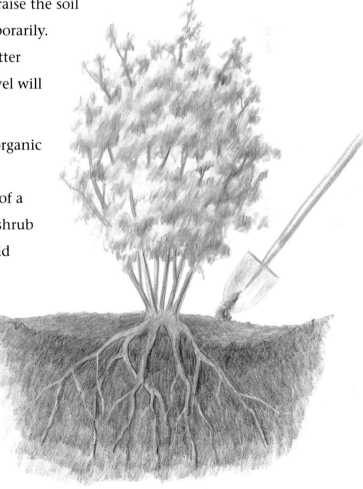

To check your soil texture quickly, simply squeeze some lightly moist soil in your hand.

with wooden siding or fencing that isn't rot-resistant.

• When planting around existing trees, shrubs, and perennial flowers, avoid covering the crown—where stems emerge from the ground—with organic material. This helps prevent disease problems.

■ Test your soil by feel before and after it is amended to judge the extent of the change. Take a small handful of lightly moist soil from several inches below the soil surface. Squeeze it into a ball in your hand and watch the results when you extend your fingers. Sandy soils, which can have a scratchy feel, will fall apart. To enrich a sandy soil, apply and incorporate a several-inch layer of compost and even an inch or two of clay, then try again. When the soil is improved, the ball will cling together better.

Clay soils, which have a slick feel, will form a tight ball that's not easily broken up. To lighten clay soil, add extra compost and coarse sand. When the soil is light enough, the ball will break up with a tap of a finger.

∎ Till or spade a thick layer of compost into lightly moist (never wet) soil to bring it to life before planting a new garden. If you are starting with hard, compacted soil, it's necessary to spade the soil first to break it up. Go over the area, removing weed roots and other unwanted vegetation as you go. Then go over the soil with a rototiller. After the first pass, go over it again crosswise until you break the soil into reasonably small pieces. If your soil is really poor, see double digging on pages 27–29.

Your well-tilled soil, like screened topsoil, may look great at first, but silt or clay soils are likely to get stiff, crusty, and hard after a few

COMPOSTING

Making your own compost takes several months, so many gardeners find it easier to purchase bagged compost. Either way, compost is a good additive for soils low in organic materials. Added to clay soil, compost lightens the soil and improves aeration; added to sandy soil, compost can improve water-holding capacity.

heavy downpours. The best way to keep soil loose and light is to add organic matter.

Add a 4- to 6-inch-deep layer (more if soil is very poor) of compost to the soil and work it down until it's 10 to 12 inches deep. The soil will become darker, moister, and spongier—a dramatic conversion right before your eyes. As long as the organic matter remains in the soil, the soil is likely to stay loose. But since it slowly decays, you will have to continue to add organic matter—compost, mulch, or shredded leaves—to maintain the desired texture.

■ Try spading or no-till systems to preserve the texture and organic content of thriving garden soils. Once the soil is loose, light, and rich, minimal disturbance helps preserve the levels of organic matter. Avoid repeated tilling, which breaks healthy soil clumps and speeds up decay.

Instead of tilling, loosen rich soil before planting by turning the surface shallowly with a shovel and breaking it apart with a smack from the shovel backside. Very loose soil can be made ready for direct seeding by combing it with a hoe or cultivator.

Double-dig a garden bed intended for deep-rooted plants such as roses.

DOUBLE DIGGING

Double-digging garden beds to make high-performance gardens for deep-rooted plants such as roses and perennials is a tradition in many beautiful British gardens. The average rototiller works the soil only 8 or 10 inches deep and won't break up compacted soil below. Double-digging will.

Use your shovel to turn the soil below it (likely to be one of the heaviest parts of the job) and break it up. Another (sometimes easier) option is to jab a garden fork (like a big pitchfork) into the hard lower soil and rock it around until the soil breaks up. If organic matter is needed, you should add it to the lower level at this point.

■ Double-digging requires a bit of a stiff upper lip, because it takes a lot of manual labor. Do a little at a time so you don't overdo it, or hire a professional landscaper if you have health restrictions.

■ Start with vacant soil that is stripped of grass and other vegetation. Beginning at one end of the garden, remove a strip of soil a spade's length deep and a spade's width wide. Put it in a wheelbarrow.

■ Do the same thing to the second strip of soil next to the first row. But turn the surface topsoil into the first trench, adding organic matter as desired. Then loosen and amend the exposed subsurface soil. Continue filling each trench from the adjacent row and loosening the soil below. Fill the final strip with the soil from the wheelbarrow.

RAISED BEDS

Build raised beds where the soil is too hard, rocky, poor, or wet for plants to grow well. Instead of struggling to change these bad conditions, construct a great garden bed over them.

In vegetable gardens, simply mound up planting rows 6 to 8 inches high and 2 to 3 feet wide. (You can walk in the paths beside the planting rows without compressing the raised soil.) Set permanent and decorative gardens in handsome raised-bed frames built of timbers, logs, rocks, or bricks, which can vary from 4 inches to 4 feet high. Don't hesitate to ask for professional help with big building projects, which need strong structures if you want them to last.

TIME-SAVING TIP

Pile dug-out earth on a tarp instead of on the grass when digging a hole for planting or excavating a garden pool. You can easily drag away any excess soil, and you won't have to rake up little clods trapped in the turf. Don't waste that soil. You can use it to build a waterfall beside the pool or to fill a raised bed for herbs or vegetables.

A raised bed garden is a good alternative where the soil isn't usable.

SHEDDING SOME LIGHT ON LIGHT

Many plants, especially lawn grass, flowers, roses, vegetables, fruit trees, and conifers (needle-leaved evergreens) thrive in bright sun, which provides abundant energy for growth, flowering, and fruiting. But some plants, particularly those native to forests and glens, need shadier conditions. Learn the sun requirements of any plant you intend to grow so you can put it in the right place.

ASSESSING LIGHT CONDITIONS

■ Watch how sunlight and shadows hit the ground to determine how much shade exists during the growing season under deciduous trees (those that drop their leaves in fall). This test helps you determine which shade-loving plants will thrive there. Some suggested plants for varying degrees of shade are found in the list on page 36.

- Full shade is found under thickly branched trees or evergreens. A garden that's located here will receive little or no direct sun and remain gloomily lit. Only a limited number of plants are suitable for this situation. You should choose flowers and ferns with evergreen leaves.

- Partial shade is found under trees that allow sunlight to penetrate through the canopy and dapple the ground throughout the day. A garden grown under a lightly branched honey locust tree would fall into this category. A larger selection of plants are capable of growing under these conditions than in full shade.

The shade in your yard determines which plants can grow well there.

With full sun in the morning and dappled sun and shade the rest of the day, many showy perennials will grow successfully.

• Light shade is found in places where plants are in direct sun for a portion of the day. This could be found in a garden under mature trees with tall barren trunks. The sun can shine in under the high leafy canopies. Light-shade conditions also exist on the east or west side of a wall or building. Here you can grow many shade-loving plants as well as shade-tolerant plants, which are sun-lovers capable of growing moderately well in light shade.

• Providing a minimum of 6 to 8 hours of direct sun a day is sufficient for most plants that need full sun. The term "full sun" doesn't actually mean plants must be in bright light every moment of the day, only most of the day. The minimum must be met, however, even during the shorter days of spring and fall for perennials, trees, and shrubs.

LIGHTEN UP: MAKING THE MOST OF THE SUN

■ Try exposing flowering shade plants to a half day of morning sun to encourage better blooming. Extra light can also keep the plants more compact, tidy, and self-supporting.

■ Grow sun-loving spring bulbs and wildflowers beneath deciduous shade trees to make the most of the sun before the tree leaves emerge. This is a great strategy if you have a shady yard and therefore have trouble getting flowers to grow during summer and fall. Crocuses, squills, Spanish bluebells, daffodils, wind-flowers, glory-of-the-snow, and wildflowers such as bloodroot, squirrel corn, and other local natives thrive in spring sun. When tree leaves emerge and the setting grows dark, many of these spring growers fall dormant and lie quietly below the ground until spring sun arrives again.

These spring flowers will thrive until the leaves of the tree above them begin to expand.

■ Paint a dark wall white to reflect more light onto plants. Just like the silver solar reflectors used by sunbathers to intensify their tans, a light-colored wall reflects additional light onto nearby plants. Similarly, using a mulch of white pebbles, sand, or gravel will reflect light up through the bottom of plants, a technique often used in gardens of Mediterranean herbs or silver-leaved plants that thrive on plenty of sun.

■ Limb-up trees or remove smaller, scraggly, or unwanted saplings and brush to brighten a densely shaded spot. Tall, mature shade trees can have their lower limbs removed (a heavy job

SOME PLANTS FOR SUNNY CONDITIONS

Broad-Leaf Evergreens: boxwood, holly, waxmyrtle

Conifers: pines, spruces, firs, junipers, false cypress, yews, arborvitae

Trees: maples, oaks, elms, magnolias, crab apples, hawthorns, apples, pears, peaches, plums

Shrubs: roses, viburnum, potentilla, spirea, lilacs

Perennials: yarrow, sea thrift, Shasta daisies, chrysanthemums, coreopsis, pinks, coneflowers, blanketflowers

Annuals: portulaca, gazania, gerbera, marigolds, zinnias, dahlias

Herbs: lavender, thyme, sage, rosemary

requiring a professional arborist) to produce light shade. For even more light, arborists can thin out overcrowded branches in the canopy, leaving some openings in the foliage for sun penetration.

Removing unwanted tangles of young trees, wild shrubs, and other woody growth is a project you can do yourself. Look for self-sown seedlings around trees such as maples, oaks, ashes, and elms. Crab apples will send up vertical sprouts called *suckers,* turning the tree into a shrub. Get a pair of long-handled pruning lopers to trim out the smaller growth and a pruning saw to

SOME PLANTS FOR SHADY CONDITIONS

Plants for full shade:

- Ferns, pachysandra, barrenwort

Plants for partial shade:

- Spring wildflowers: trout lilies, bloodroot, bellworts, Solomon's seal
- Shrubs: rhododendrons, azaleas, hydrangea
- Shade-loving perennials: bleeding heart, hostas, mint, bergenia, sweet woodruff, astilbes
- Annuals: impatiens, browallia

Plants for light shade:

- Annuals: begonias, coleus, ageratum, sweet alyssum
- Herbs: basil, parsley, bee balm
- Vegetables: lettuce, spinach, arugula
- Perennials: daylilies, hostas, anemones, hardy geraniums, coral bells, lobelia

remove larger trunks. When finished, you can admire the newly revealed shape of the tree trunk and the ferns, hostas, and other shade plants that can grow beneath it. Be sure not to overthin; you should leave enough saplings to replace older trees as they die.

■ Prune low-hanging branches on a sunny day so you can see how the light changes. This way you can watch the shade lighten. You also can keep an eye on the shadows, which will dance from one side of the tree to the other, changing with the time of day and position of the sun. Their silhouettes can be a beautiful part of the garden, especially in winter when the dark shadows stand out on the white snow.

■ Do not prune oaks in summer. Even though this may be when you are anxious to lighten shade the most, it will make your trees susceptible to oak wilt disease. Prune, instead, in late winter.

SUN INTENSITY

Consider differences in sun intensity when planting on the east and west side of shade-casting trees or buildings. Even if east- and west-facing sites receive the same number of hours of sun, they will not produce identical results.

■ Gardens with an eastern exposure are illuminated with cool morning sun, then shaded in the afternoon. They

Consider sun exposure when planting directly against the house.

are ideal locations for minimizing heat stress in southern climates or for plants such as rhododendrons that can burn in hot sun.

■ Gardens with western exposure are shaded in the morning and drenched in hot sun in the afternoon. Sunburn, bleaching, and sometimes death of delicate leaves can result, especially in warm climates and when growing sensitive young or shade-loving plants. Afternoon sun can also cause brightly colored flowers to fade. However, the west side of a building is the ideal place for sun-loving and drought-tolerant plants.

INDOORS

When growing potted plants indoors, supplement natural light with fluorescent or grow lights. Sometimes in winter the weather may be cloudy for days, even weeks. This creates problems for tropical plants, potted flowers, and even foliage plants that need light to remain healthy.

The solution is to hang a fluorescent shop light directly over your indoor plants. Special grow lights or full spectrum bulbs (formulated to produce light wavelengths that plants need most) can be used in place of fluorescent bulbs for spectacular results with flowering plants. For extra-easy maintenance, plug the lights into an automatic timer, then set them to turn on for 14 to 16 hours a day and off again at night.

Indoor potted plants may require a supplemental light source.

THE WAYS OF WATER

Without water, plants wilt and die. But too much water can be as bad for plants as not enough. If land plants are submerged in water for too long—even if just their roots are submerged—they may rot or drown from lack of oxygen.

Balancing plants' water needs is like having a healthful diet. Everything should be consumed in moderation. Provide your plants with enough water for good health, but don't flood them with it.

How and when you water your plants can make a big difference.

WATERING GUIDELINES

- Apply water in the cool of the morning or evening when the wind is calm and water loss through evaporation is minimal.

- Avoid watering disease-susceptible plants at night. If water sits on plant foliage for hours, it can encourage fungal diseases to attack leaves, buds, flowers, and fruit. Plants susceptible to leaf spots, fruit rots, and flower blights are best watered in the morning, when the warming sun will quickly dry the leaves and discourage fungus development.

- Provide an inch of water a week for many plants and lawn grasses. The idea is to keep the soil lightly moist and to prevent it from drying out completely, which would be damaging to most plants. But because plants don't always follow the rules, there are exceptions to this general guideline:

• More water may be necessary if you have hot weather, dry sandy soil, or

crowded intensive plantings or containers.

• When the weather is cool, the plants are widely spaced, or the soil is heavy and moisture-retentive, less water may be required.

• Young or new plantings require more moisture at the soil surface to help their roots get established. You should water more often to accommodate their needs.

• Mature plantings with large root systems can be watered heavily and less often than younger plants. The moisture soaks deep into the soil and encourages the roots to thrive.

■ Set a rain gauge in an open area of the garden to learn how much water the garden receives each week. You can purchase an inexpensive one at a garden center. After each rainfall, check the depth of the rain inside. A commercial rain gauge is calibrated and easy to read. Judge the need for supplemental irrigation accordingly.

Rain gauges are also helpful when trying to determine when you have watered enough with an overhead sprinkler. Since some sprinklers apply water unevenly (more up close and less farther out), you could set several rain gauges around the garden and compare the amount of moisture each one collects. If the readings vary widely, move the sprinkler more frequently or invest in a more efficient model.

HOSES

■ Stretch soaker hoses through the garden to provide water directly to plant roots. Soaker hoses are made of water-permeable fabrics, perforated recycled rubber, or other porous materials. When attached to a hose with the water turned on low or medium, moisture droplets weep out along the length of the hose. Very little evaporates and none sprays on plant foliage, helping discourage diseases. But it may take an hour or more depending on your soil.

■ Soaker hoses require a little special attention in order to work properly. Here are some hints:

- Soaker hoses work best at low pressure (10 psi). If you have high pressure, consider a pressure regulator or flow reducer for optimal performance.

- Run soaker hoses straight through the garden. If set to turn or curve too sharply, they will kink and won't fill with water.

- Expect more water to be released from the far end of the faucet and less to be released from the closest end.

- If the hose is moistening only one side of a plant root system, move the hose to water the dry side before you consider the job done.

PLANTS TO WATER IN THE MORNING, NOT AT NIGHT

Roses

Apples

Pears

Peaches

Plums

Cherries

Grapes

Strawberries

Raspberries

Blackberries

Tomatoes

Cucumbers

Melons

Beans

Begonias

Geraniums

Peonies

Dahlias

Chrysanthemums

It's best to water grapes in the morning so that fruit clusters dry out during the day.

• To determine if the soil has been watered enough, dig into the soil beside the hose. If the water has seeped 12 inches down, it's about time to turn off the hose. Remember how long this took for the next time around.

• For faster results, look for flat hoses that are peppered with small holes. Of course there's a trade-off: These hoses do provide water more quickly, but they are not as gentle on the soil.

• If you like soaker hose results, you can upgrade to permanent or semipermanent drip irrigation systems. Although more expensive, these systems are custom-designed for varying soil types and individual plant water needs. They also don't require shuffling around the garden.

■ Wheel hose carts around the yard instead of dragging armloads of hoses and causing wear and tear on your back. Hose carts consist of a reel with a crank that you can use to neatly coil the hose, eliminating tangles, knots,

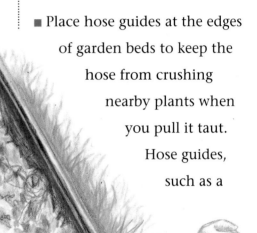

and kinks. This reel is set on a two- or four-wheeled base with a handle for easy pulling. Look for large-wheeled types if you're rolling the cart over the lawn or rough ground. Smaller wheels are fine on a paved path or patio.

■ Place hose guides at the edges of garden beds to keep the hose from crushing nearby plants when you pull it taut. Hose guides, such as a wooden stake pounded into the ground at an outward angle, prevent the hose from sliding into the garden. Decorative hose guides (stakes carved like animals, elves, or flowers) can be found at some garden centers, mail-order garden suppliers, or craft shows. You could also improvise by using things like plastic pink flamingos, garden statues, or birdbaths.

■ Use a water breaker on the end of your hose to change heavy water flow into a gentle sprinkle. This helps prevent soil compaction and spreads the water more evenly across planting areas. Put an adjustable spray nozzle on the end of the hose, watering only with the setting that produces fine droplets in a gentle spray and wide arc. Save the strong blasts for washing the car.

Or, look for spray heads developed specifically for garden use. Some are set on angled bases, making it easy to reach in between plants. Others are on long poles for watering hanging baskets.

Water breakers should be put on watering cans, too, especially when watering young plants such as seedlings, which can be broken or uprooted with a strong drenching.

CONSERVING WATER

■ Use gray water on potted plants or small gardens to reduce water use. Gray water is the leftover tap water from activities such as rinsing vegetables at the kitchen sink. Be sure to avoid water contaminated with water-softener salts, harsh detergents, fats, oils, or other extras that would harm plants. Gray water has been used successfully in arid parts of the United States and is well worth using anywhere. It helps prevent stress on wells during drought and lowers utility bills for people with municipal water lines.

Capture gray water in a basin stored close to the sink, where it will be handy to pull out and use. Transfer the gray water to a watering can before watering potted plants or new plantings. A little moisture in

a time of need will make a big difference.

■ Catch water from a downspout into a container. This unfluoridated, unchlorinated water is ideal for watering plants. It comes at an ambient temperature, not shockingly cold from the tap—which is hard on warmth-loving plants. And perhaps best of all—at least from the gardener's perspective—it's free!

The easiest way to collect downspout runoff is to put a container at the bottom of the downspout. A topless bucket or barrel with a sturdy spigot at the bottom can be set in place permanently. Simply drain the water from the spigot into your watering can. To handle larger quantities of water, look for a 30- to 50-gallon barrel or drum. It's helpful to keep a large

Grouping water-loving plants together looks beautiful and natural and makes your job easier.

MOISTURE-LOVING PLANTS

Louisiana, Siberian, and
 Japanese irises

Foamflowers

Marsh marigolds

Solomon's seal

Sweet flag

Horsetails

Swamp hibiscus

Cardinal flower

Impatiens

Hostas

Ferns

Joe-pye weed

Astilbes

Umbrella plant

Ligularia

Mint

Cordgrass

Willows

cup or other dipper on hand for transferring the water into a watering can.

You can tap every downspout around your house for maximum water yield or, if you prefer, just use the downspouts in the private parts of the landscape, the back and side yards. Be sure to cap containers so that birds, small mammals, and reptiles do not fall in and drown.

■ Another option is to redirect runoff from downspouts into flower beds or lawn. Flexible tubing can be connected to the end of the downspout and directed into nearby plantings around the foundation of the house or to flower or vegetable gardens. For maximum benefits, shape beds like a shallow bowl to collect the water and give it time to soak in. Or, as an alternative, the garden could be made fairly level with lower moisture-gathering saucers made around newly planted trees or shrubs or plants with high moisture needs.

In dry climates, the tubing can be covered with soil or mulch and kept connected all the time. In climates with periods of overly wet weather, the tubing should be disconnected during soggy seasons to prevent oversaturation of the soil, which may cause plants to rot, unless you are growing water-loving plants like Siberian iris and primrose.

■ Drop the soil level in the boulevard strip, the row of grass between the sidewalk and the street, so it will collect runoff rainwater that otherwise would be lost to street sewers or roadside ditches. A small 1- to 2-inch drop in soil level will be enough to do the job. If planting sod, make the soil level even lower to account for the extra height of sod roots. In cold climates, you may have to remove sand or grit that can accumulate after winter snowplowing to maintain an appropriate height.

Garden Care

L ike playing a lively game of tennis, keeping your garden looking great depends on having the right equipment, developing a good technique, and being organized enough to do the right things at the right times. This may sound like a lot to juggle, but once you understand the basics, it's easy.

MAINTENANCE AND PRUNING

GARDEN TOOLS

For a start, you'll need good hoes, spades, rakes, pruners, and a sturdy wheelbarrow. Buy the best tools you can afford. There is no substitute for good tools. Tools that cost half the price but last only two years (instead of 22 years) are not cost-effective in the long run. They may also fail you in the middle of a big project, just when you need them most.

Once your garden soil is in good condition, small hand tools are right for many tasks.

Many garden tasks can be accomplished with just a round-point shovel (second from bottom), a drain spade (top), and trowels of various sizes.

∎ One way to ensure good quality is to buy tools from a reputable dealer willing to guarantee their performance. For another quality test, look at the way tools are made. Tools with steel blades are strong enough to last for years without bending. Stainless steel is even better, because it won't rust. Spades, shovels, and forks with hard ash handles are unlikely to splinter or break in the middle of a heavy operation.

∎ Hand pruning shears are used for small stems under about a half-inch in diameter. Look for scissor-type blades, which make sharper, cleaner cuts than the anvil type with a sharp blade pressing on a flat blade. Also check out new ergonomically designed pruning shears that minimize repetitive motion stress. There are even shears made especially for left-handed gardeners.

- Loppers are long-handled pruning shears with larger blades for cutting branches up to about 1½ inches in diameter. Pruning is easier if you buy a model with ratcheting action for more power with less effort.

- Pruning saws should have narrow blades, be easy to maneuver into tight spaces, and be toothed on one side only.

- People with smaller builds can find specially designed tools with smaller blades and shorter handles, which are easier to control than oversized tools.

- Keep hand tools in a basket on the garage or pantry shelf so they are always easy to find. Nothing is more frustrating than seeing a branch in need of a quick trim but having to search all over the house and garage for a pair of pruning shears. If all your tools are kept together— and returned to their proper place after each use—simple

Keep small maintenance tasks simple—hand tools stored in a basket are always accessible and are easy to transport.

garden projects will stay quick and uncomplicated.

■ Always set hoes, soil rakes, and other tools with horizontal teeth or blades facedown on the ground when not being used. If stepped on, the teeth or blades sink harmlessly into the soil. But if left upright, an unwary walker might step on the teeth, making the tool tip and the handle spring up into his or her face.

■ To keep tools upright and organized, attach a topless and bottomless coffee can or similarly shaped plastic container to the top of a fence post, securing it with wire. You can slip in the handles of

rakes, shovels, and hoes, keeping them together and out from underfoot.

■ Keep a bucket of clean sand and machine oil in the garage to cure tools after each use. This is particularly helpful for rust-prone digging instruments such as shovels, garden forks, and hoes. After

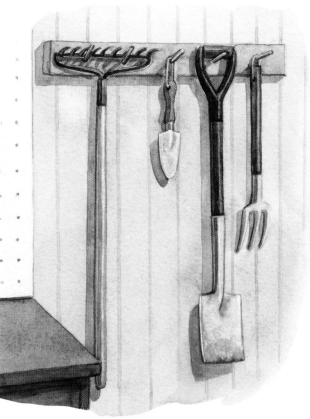

Many annual weeds germinate in autumn, so keep your soil mulched all season.

use, rinse tools with water and dry the blades. Then insert them in the oil/sand mixture. The sand will scour off debris, and the oil will coat the metal, retarding rust.

MULCHING

Cover garden beds with a layer of mulch to keep weeds down and reduce the need for water. Annual weed seeds are less likely to sprout when the soil is covered with enough mulch to keep the soil surface in the dark.

When it comes to water, even a thin layer of mulch—nature's moisturizer—will reduce evaporation from the soil surface. Thicker mulches can reduce water use by as much as 50 percent.

■ Mulches vary in their appearance, makeup, and texture, which will influence how you use them. Here are some examples:

- Varying appearances: For a soothing, natural-looking garden, use dark-colored organic mulches made of bark or compost. For a brilliant-looking garden, consider a mulch of bright gravel. In utilitarian gardens such as vegetable gardens, straw makes an excellent mulch. Avoid colored mulch or beauty bark.

- Soil improvement: This calls for the use of organic mulches that break down to add organic matter to the soil.

- Texture: For maximum effectiveness with only a thin mulch layer, look for fine-textured mulches such as twice-shredded bark, compost, or cocoa hulls.

For an airy mulch, try thicker layers of coarse-textured mulches such as straw or bark chunks.

■ Kill off sod or dense weeds by layering newspaper, alone or with a thick layer of compost or mulch, directly on the garden site. This treatment cuts off the sunlight to unwanted vegetation, which will eventually decay and add organic matter to the garden. The newspaper decomposes, too. (What a bargain!)

■ Mulch new plants with straw or chopped leaves after planting in the fall to prevent root damage during winter. A little mulch used immediately after planting can help to keep the soil moist and encourage continued root growth.

But the main reason to mulch lies ahead, in winter. Alternately freezing and thawing, expanding and contracting soil can break new roots or even push new plantings out of the ground, a process called *frost heaving.* By mulching generously with an airy material like straw when the soil first freezes, you can help keep the soil frozen until winter ends, at which point the mulch can be removed.

Use loppers on branches up to 1½ inches thick.

■ In winter, mulch evergreen perennials and ground covers with evergreen boughs to protect them from winter burn (the cold-weather opposite of sunburn). When the soil is frozen, the wind is strong, and the sun is bright, moisture is pulled out of the vulnerable leaves and cannot be replaced by the frozen roots. A protective layer of evergreen boughs, possibly obtained by recycling the branches of a Christmas tree, forms a protective shield over vulnerable greenery. Straw will also do the job, especially in colder areas where there is less chance of rot in winter.

Celebrate if you live in a snowy area. Snow is the best mulch of all, and it may allow you to grow plants that won't survive winter in snowless areas farther south.

PRUNING

A few basic pruning cuts will help you rejuvenate and control the size of your shrubs and trees. Prune with top-quality pruning shears, loppers, and a saw. Sharp blades and sturdy handles can make pruning a breeze. Dull blades—rusty and sticking—make projects harder than they need to be. They can also cause wood to be crushed or torn, which is damaging to the plant. Look for hard, durable blades capable of being resharpened and a sturdy, smoothly operating nut hold-ing the blades together. Hand shears should also have a safety latch to keep the blades closed when not in use.

∎ Candle-prune pines to control their size or make them branch more thickly. Candle-pruning (also called *candling*) refers to manipulating the candle-shape new shoots that arise in spring. When the candle is fully elongated but

Hand pruning shears work well on smaller stems.

before the needles enlarge, use your pruning shears to cut off a little, half, or most of the soft candle, depending on how much you want to limit size. The cut should slant at an angle instead of slicing straight across the candle. Come the following spring, clusters of new side branches will appear. Continue candling each year for more dramatic results.

Candling is especially handy for keeping mugo pines small enough for use near the house or in a mixed border. It also can help lanky, open-

branched pines fill in to form a more solid and substantial cone.

■ Renewal-prune flowering shrubs by removing one-third of the stems once each year. This modest effort acts like a fountain of youth, keeping these shrubs young. It's much better than shearing, which reduces flowering, has to be repeated frequently, and can even accelerate aging.

Spring-blooming shrubs like rhododendron can be pruned after they finish blooming.

Use pruning loppers or a pruning saw to cut the oldest stems off at the ground, ideally in early spring before the shrubs break dormancy. This timing encourages quick renewal, but a few spring flowers will be sacrificed on early bloomers. If you can't bear that thought, wait to prune until after flowering. As spring and summer progress, new branches will take the place of the old branches. If pruned every year, the shrub will be continually rejuvenated, remaining healthy and beautiful.

Cut worn-out shrubs to the ground to rejuvenate them or thin them out.

■ Rejuvenate tired, overgrown, or weak shrubs by cutting them to the ground. Although this may sound like giving up, just the opposite is true. It can be the start of a whole new shrub. This technique works well with easy-growing shrubs such as lilacs, viburnums, and butterfly bushes but is generally not effective with evergreen shrubs (except boxwoods). The idea is similar to renewal-pruning, only more radical. It should be done in early spring before leaves or flowers emerge. Shrubs with strong root systems will resprout with a fountain of new stems. So that they don't crowd each other, you should thin excessively thick clumps to allow the strongest to continue growing and form the foundation for the new shrub.

Shrubs with weak root systems or disease problems may not resprout. If there are no signs of life a month or two after cutting the shrub back, start looking for a replacement plant.

■ Prune to the outside of a tree's branch collar for fast healing and good tree health. The branch collar is the swelling located at the base of the branch, where it arises from another limb or the trunk. The branch collar is like a hospital isolation ward; it houses protective chemicals that help keep diseases from invading the parent limb. When removing a branch for any reason, leaving that branch collar in place shuts out any passing pathogens.

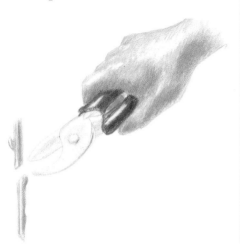

■ Slant pruning cuts away from the bud to encourage water to run off. This helps keep the bud healthy so it can grow and prosper.

STAKING

Use wire grid supports instead of individual stakes to easily hold up bushy but floppy perennials such as peonies. You can buy commercial grid supports, which are handsome round or square grids neatly set on legs; green grids are more camouflaged amid the foliage than metallic grids. Or you can make your own grid supports out of a sheet of wire mesh, cut a little wider than the plant it will support. The extra length can be bent into legs.

The supporting process takes one simple step. Set the grid over a newly emerging perennial in spring. The stems will grow up through it, retaining their natural shape while staying firmly upright.

The alternative (which occurs when you let the plant sprawl before staking it) is more difficult and less attractive. Corsetting the drooping limbs with twine and hoisting them up with a stake of wood can result in broken stems and a miserable-looking specimen.

PERENNIALS THAT OFTEN NEED SUPPORT

Asters

Balloon flowers

Bellflowers (taller types)

Garden phlox

Hollyhocks

Foxgloves

Pyrethrum daisies

Sedums (taller types)

Shasta daisies

Yarrows

PESTS AND OTHER PROBLEMS

PREVENTING DISEASE

Growing healthy plants is the first step toward a great garden. To achieve this, it's important to prevent disease by paying careful attention to plant selection, planting, and care.

■ Choose disease-resistant cultivars whenever possible. They are bred to resist infection—an ideal way to avoid diseases. Growing disease-resistant vegetables prevents chemical tainting of your food. Disease-resistant varieties of popular flowers such as roses save you time, trouble, and expense.

There are varying levels of protection available:

• Some cultivars have multiple disease resistances for maximum protection. The 'Big Beef' tomato, for instance, resists various types of wilts: tobacco mosaic virus, nematodes, and gray leaf spot. Little is left that can harm it.

Many tomatoes are specifically bred to resist disease.

SOME DISEASE-RESISTANT CULTIVARS

Apples: 'Liberty,' 'Jonafree,' 'MacFree,' 'Freedom'

Beans: 'Florence,' 'Buttercrisp,' 'Jade'

Cucumbers: 'Park's All-Season Burpless Hybrid,' 'Fancipack,' 'Homemade Pickles,' 'Tasty King,' 'Sweet Success,' 'Salad Bush'

Peas: 'Super Sugar Snap,' 'Sugar Pop,' 'Maestro,' 'Green Arrow'

Roses: 'The Fairy,' 'Red Fairy,' rugosa roses, 'Carefree Delight,' David Austin English Roses, Town and Country Roses, Meidiland roses

Strawberries: 'Surecrop,' 'Cavendish,' 'Redchief,' 'Allstar,' 'Guardian,' 'Scott,' 'Lateglow,' 'Delite'

Tomatoes: 'Celebrity,' 'Better Boy,' 'LaRossa,' 'Enchantment,' 'Sunmaster,' 'Mountain Delight,' 'Big Beef,' 'Beefmaster,' 'Sweet Million,' 'Viva Italia,' 'Roma'

Zinnias: 'Star Gold,' 'Star Orange,' 'Star White,' 'Crystal White,' 'Cherry Pinwheel,' 'Salmon Pinwheel,' 'Rose Pinwheel,' 'Orange Pinwheel'

- Some cultivars resist only one disease. But if that disease is a problem in your area, then these plants will be worth their weight in gold.

- Other plants are disease-tolerant, meaning they may still get the disease but should grow well despite it.

Bee balm is often susceptible to powdery mildew, so select a resistant cultivar or spray with wilt-proofing solution.

To find out more about disease-resistant cultivars for your area, consult your local Cooperative Extension Service or a knowledgeable professional grower. Or get your name on the mailing list for nursery and seed catalogs that describe disease-resistant cultivars.

■ Spray plants susceptible to foliage fungus with wilt-proofing solution before disease strikes. This product is a pine oil modified to spread into a film coating that protects evergreen foliage from drying out during winter. An unexpected side effect of the film is that it keeps fungus spores from penetrating into susceptible leaves. Mix according to label directions and try it on phlox, bee balm, cucumbers, watermelons, tomatoes, and apples.

Pair disease-resistant varieties with good garden practices to reduce pest and disease problems.

■ Experiment with baking soda sprays to prevent fungus diseases. Mix 2 teaspoons baking soda in 2 quarts water with ½ teaspoon corn oil. Shake well, put in a sprayer, and go to work. Spray susceptible plants often and always after rain to help keep diseases such as powdery mildew from getting started.

■ Thin the stems of disease-prone plants to improve air circulation. Mildew-susceptible phlox and bee balm, for instance, can grow into clumps so thick that they block airflow. This encourages fungus attack, but it is easily corrected. When new growth is coming up in the spring, cut out every third stem, targeting those that are weak or in areas of the thickest growth.

PREVENTING PESTS

■ Interplant herbs and flowers with vegetables to help reduce pest problems. This gives the vegetable garden a colorful patchwork look and helps confuse problem pests. The varied aromas of inter-plantings make it hard for pests to find their favorite food by scent. This works particularly well if you interplant with powerfully fragrant herbs and flowers such as mints, basils, lemon geraniums, garlic, or onions.

■ Attract beneficial insects. Sprinkling flowering plants amid the garden helps draw ladybugs, spiders, lacewings, and tiny parasitic wasps who prey on plant-eating pests. The flowers provide shelter plus nectar and pollen, an alternative food source.

Once beneficial insects are at home in your garden, keep them there. Remember, they can be killed as quickly as plant pests by broad-spectrum pesticides, which kill indiscriminately. It's best to

Interplanting adds color and texture to the garden—and also deters pests.

avoid pesticides or use targeted pesticides such as Bt (a bacterial disease of caterpillars that won't harm other insects) to protect beneficial insects.

Ladybugs are beneficial insects.

■ Use floating row covers to keep pests off vegetables. This simple idea works so well it's a wonder nobody thought of it years ago. Floating row covers are lightweight fabrics that you can drape over plants. They allow sun, rain, and fresh air to penetrate, but if secured to the ground with rocks, bricks, or long metal staples, they will keep flying insects out. Here are some great ways to use floating row covers:

• Eliminate maggots (fly larvae), which will tunnel into the roots of radishes, turnips, carrots, onions, and other vegetables. Row covers keep egg-laying female flies away from the vegetables. If there are no eggs, there are no maggots.

Floating row covers let sun, rain, and air get through while keeping plants safe from pests.

- Keep potato beetles from eating the foliage off potato leaves and vines. Pin the row cover edges down tightly so the beetles can't crawl under.

- Protect cucumbers, squash, and pumpkins from cucumber beetles, which carry a wilt disease capable of killing entire vines. Since flowers of these vines need insect pollination for fruit set, the covers must be lifted for several hours at least every other day for bees to do their work.

■ Use barriers of copper strips or diatomaceous earth to keep slugs away from plants. Slugs are voracious plant eaters. They eat almost anything, ganging up on tender succulent plants and eating them down to the ground. They thrive where soils are damp, spending sunny days under rocks, logs, or mulch and coming out to eat when it's rainy or cool and dark. Any slug-control measures you use will work better if you clear out excess mulch and any dark, dank hiding places where slugs might breed.

• Diatomaceous earth is a gritty substance that pierces the skin of soft-bodied slugs. Sprinkle it on the soil, encircling plants

Use sticky red balls for control of apple maggots on apple and plum trees.

plagued by slugs. Use horticultural-grade diatomaceous earth, not the kind sold in swimming pool stores.

• Copper strips, set around the edge of the garden, prevent slug trespass by creating an unpleasant reaction when touched with the mucus on the crawling slugs. Set copper strips an inch deep and several inches high, so that slugs can't get over or under.

■ Kill existing slugs by trapping them in deep saucers of beer. Slugs love beer, and that can be their downfall. Bury an empty plastic margarine tub in the garden soil. The top rim should be level with the soil surface. Fill the tub with beer (any kind will do) and leave it overnight. The slugs will crawl in and drown. Empty the tub every day or two and refill with beer until the tub comes through the night empty.

■ Spray aphids off plants with a strong stream of water. Aphids, small sap-sucking insects with soft, pear-shape bodies, cling to succulent young stems and buds. They reproduce quickly, sometimes covering stems that curl and distort in protest. Because aphids can multiply into swarms almost overnight, it's important to eliminate any that you find. This method works best on mature or woody plants that won't be damaged by the force of the water blast. Repeat every couple of days or any time you see new aphids arriving.

■ Deer can be a nuisance. Use bags of soap or human hair to repel deer. They seem to enjoy dining on cultivated plants and are worst in the winter, gobbling evergreens when their native food supply dwindles. But they are also a problem in spring and summer, when they like to munch tender flowers and new growth. In fall, males rub their antlers on wood and can damage small trees and shrubs.

Deer don't enjoy strong-smelling soaps and human hair so this is one way to repel them. Simply stuff powerfully scented soap in a mesh bag and dangle it from branches about 3 feet high. You also can set soap bars directly on the ground. Replenish the soap supply frequently so it won't dissolve away or lose its smell. You can also fill mesh bags

This deer may look cute, but it's a nuisance in the garden.

SOME PLANTS PREFERRED BY DEER
(Based on Cornell Cooperative Extension Service research)

Apples	Phlox
Arborvitaes	Plums
European mountain ash	Lilies
Asters	Redbud
Evergreen azaleas	Rhododendrons
Cherries	Hybrid tea rose
Clematis	Tulips
Fraser and balsam firs	Winged euonymus
Hostas	Wintercreeper
English ivy	Yews
Norway maple	Daylilies

with human hair. Hang them outside (like a furry scarecrow) so deer wonder if you are hiding in the garden. Refill bags as soon as you pull another handful from your hairbrush. If deer are a chronic problem, consider spraying plants with deterrents or erecting a fence.

Organic gardening places an emphasis on healthy soil to ensure healthy plants.

ORGANIC GARDENING TECHNIQUES

Organic gardeners shun the use of synthetic chemicals to keep their yards free from potential hazards. But the real success of organic gardens lies in the methods used to keep plants growing vigorously, without a heavy reliance on sprays. Organic gardening cuts right to the heart of the matter: soil.

Soil is the life force of the garden. When enriched with organic matter, the soil becomes moist, fertile, and friable—ideal for healthy plants. It also nourishes a rich population of beneficial organisms such as earthworms and nutrient-releasing bacteria. And it harbors root-extending fungi that help make growing conditions optimal.

■ Make compost the lazy way by layering leaves, lawn clippings, and kitchen waste.

COMPOST BLENDS

Organic material decays most quickly if blended with approximately equal parts of the following:

Nitrogen-Rich Soft and Green Material

- Manure from chickens, cows, horses, rabbits, pigs, guinea pigs, and other herbivores
- Fruit and vegetable peels
- Grass clippings
- Green leaves
- Strips of turf
- Alfalfa

Carbon-Rich Brown and Hard Material

- Wood chips
- Ground-up twigs
- Sawdust
- Pruning scraps
- Autumn leaves
- Straw

Then simply leave it until it's ready. Nature's recyclers will take organic matter no matter how it is presented and turn it into rich, dark compost. This process just takes longer in an untended pile.

To begin your compost heap, dump yard scraps in a far corner of the yard. An ideal blend would be equal amounts of soft or green material (manure and fresh leaves) and brown or hard material (dead leaves and chopped twigs). Or, if you prefer, keep the compost materials neatly contained in a wooden slat or wire mesh bin. If you put an access door on the bottom of the bin, you

OPTIONAL COMPOST-MAKING EQUIPMENT

Wire composting bin

Stackable composting bin

Wooden composting bin

Vented plastic bins

Worm boxes

Compost tumbler

Compost inoculant

Garden fork

Compost thermometer

Sifting screen

can scoop out the finished compost at the bottom while the rest is still decaying.

■ Add compost starter or good garden soil to a new compost pile to help jump-start the decay of organic materials.

Compost starter, available in garden centers or from mail-order garden catalogs, contains decay-causing microorganisms. Some brands also contain nutrients, enzymes, hormones, and other stimulants that help decomposers work as fast as possible. Special formulations can be particularly helpful for hard-to-compost, woody material like wood chips and sawdust

or for quick decay of brown leaves.

Good garden or woodland soil, although not as high-tech nor as expensive as compost starter, contains native decomposers well able to tackle a compost pile. Sprinkle it among the yard scraps as you are building the pile.

■ Use perforated PVC pipes to aerate compost piles. An ideal compost pile will reach three to four feet high—big enough to get warm from the heat of

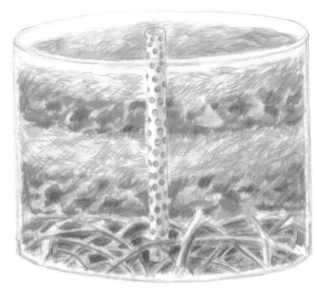

decay. Why is heat important? High temperatures—when a pile is warm enough to steam on a cool morning—semi-sterilize the developing compost, killing disease spores, hibernating pests, and weed seeds.

But the problem is that for decomposers to work efficiently enough to create heat, they need plenty of air—and not just at the surface of the pile. Aeration is traditionally provided by fluffing or turning the pile with a pitchfork, which can be hard work. But with a little advance planning and a perforated pipe, this can be avoided.

Start a compost pile on a bed of branched sticks that will allow air to rise from below. Add a perforated pipe in the center, building layers

Organic gardeners stress problem prevention in the garden. Fewer problems mean more time to relax and enjoy the garden!

Soft organic materials like kitchen scraps and discarded turf keep a compost pile active.

of old leaves, grass clippings, and other garden leftovers around it. The air will flow through the pipe into the compost pile.

■ Use on-site composting for easy soil improvement. Gather up old leaves, livestock manure, and/or green vegetable scraps and let them lie in or beside the garden until they rot, then work them into the soil. Or just heap them on the garden in the fall and till them into the soil. They will be decayed by spring. You can also dig a hole, dump in the yard waste, cover it with a little soil, and let it rot in privacy.

■ Expect to use more organic fertilizer, by volume, than synthetic chemical fertilizers. That's because organic fertilizers contain fewer nutrients by weight, averaging from 1 to about 6 or 7 percent. Contrast this with an inorganic lawn fertilizer that may contain up to 30 percent nitrogen, more than four times as much as organic fertilizer.

More is not always better when it comes to fertilizers. Lower-dose organic fertilizers are unlikely to burn plant roots or cause nutrient overdoses. Many forms release their components slowly, providing a long-term nutrient supply instead of one intense nutrient blast. Organic fertilizers may also provide a spectrum of lesser nutrients, even enzymes and hormones that can benefit growth.

For details on how to use fertilizers properly, read the package labels. The volume of fertilizer required may vary depending on the kind of plant being fertilized and the time of year.

■ Use fish emulsion fertilizer to encourage a burst of growth from new plantings, potted

flowers and vegetables, or anything that is growing a little too sluggishly for your taste. High-nitrogen fish emulsion dissolves in water and is easily absorbed and put to immediate use by the plant. For best results, follow the package directions.

■ Add toad houses to the garden to attract toads for natural pest control. Just as fairy-tale toads can be turned into handsome princes with just a kiss, ordinary toads become plant protectors just

by hopping into the garden. They may not be pretty, but toads eat plenty of bugs, so you'll be glad to see them. To encourage toads to come to live in your garden, try the following:

- Put several broken clay pots in the garden for toads to hide under.

- Water when the ground gets dry to keep the environment pleasant for amphibians.

- Avoid spraying toxic chemicals on the garden.

- Watch out for toads when tilling, hoeing, or shoveling or mowing.

■ Use organic repellents to chase away rodents and deer. Sprays made out of hot peppers, coyote or bobcat urine, rotten eggs, bonemeal, or bloodmeal—even castor oil—can make your garden

Rabbits nibble on the succulent stems of many perennials and shrubs. Use repellent sprays to deter them.

plants unappetizing to herbivores. Reapply the repellents frequently, and always after rain, to maintain high protection levels.

■ Grow French or American marigolds to kill any nematodes in the garden soil. Nematodes—microscopic wormlike pests that can damage tomatoes, potatoes, and other crops—are killed by chemicals that are released by marigold roots and decaying foliage. You can plant marigolds in and around other nematode-susceptible plants. Or just till marigolds into the soil and let them decay before planting potatoes or tomatoes.

Plant French marigolds to rid your garden of nematodes.

PROPAGATION

Starting your own plants from seeds, cuttings, divisions, and layerings saves money and expands options. But be prepared to give propagation a certain amount of attention. Young plants need tender loving care to get them off to a good start.

DIVISION OF PERENNIALS

Daylilies, hostas, astilbes, or other clump-forming perennials are easily divided with a sharp shovel. Just slice off an edge of the clump in spring or late summer. Uproot it and replant elsewhere. Keep the new division watered for at least several weeks or until it has regenerated lost roots.

Divide a large perennial clump into small divisions to get many little plants fast. This is a quick and easy way to make enough plants for the big drifts, clumps, or ground covers that are so popular in landscaping today.

A mature bee balm clump might contain 50 rooted sprouts, each of which can be separated and grown into a new plant. Other easily divided perennials include asters, daylilies, yarrow, phlox, lady's mantle, salvia, coreopsis, hardy geraniums, irises, mint, thyme, oregano, and winter savory. Here's how to make smaller divisions:

■ In spring or late summer, dig up the entire perennial plant clump and wash soil off the roots with a hose.

■ If dividing in late summer, cut back the foliage by half, or more if plants are tall and hard to handle.

■ Use your hands to break rooted sprouts into individual pieces. If roots are too hard to

work apart by hand, slice them free with a knife or pruning shears. Each section should contain at least one leafy sprout and one cluster of healthy roots.

You can grow new spider plants by potting up the attached plantlets.

■ Replant very small divisions into pots of peat-based planting mix and tend them carefully until they get a little bigger. Larger divisions can go right back into the garden if kept moist until they become reestablished.

PLANTS FROM SEED

Many plants grow well from seeds, especially annual flowers, herbs, and vegetables. You can find dozens of new, rare, or old-fashioned varieties in seed catalogs that aren't available in the local nurseries. Seed sowing allows you to grow a few, dozens, or even hundreds of seedlings from a packet costing a dollar or two. Talk about economy!

■ Keep a notebook, calendar, or advance planner to remind you when to plant seeds. For example, seeds such as tomatoes and peppers need to be planted six to eight weeks before the last spring frost, but squash and cucumbers

need to be planted only three weeks before the last spring frost. It can be hard to remember everything (and squeeze it into your schedule) unless it's written down.

Direct sowing in the garden, following directions on the packet for timing and depth of planting, is an option for those without time or space to start plants indoors.

■ Keep good propagation records to track how successful each operation has been and how the young plants are proceeding through the seasons. These records will guide you in future years. Jot down your observations weekly in a notebook. Or keep an index card on each plant you propagate so it's easy to find the next time. Some gardeners may want to computerize their records. Here are some things to note:

- How long seedlings grew indoors before being transplanted outdoors and whether that timing allowed enough, too little, or too much time for a great performance outdoors.

- When you planted seedlings outdoors and how well they responded to the weather conditions at that time.

- When the first shoots of perennial flowers and herbs emerged in spring and were ready to divide.

HARVESTING SEEDS

■ Watch the color of ripening seedpods, which is the clue to when seeds are ripe. When dry pods turn from bright green to dull green or brown and succulent fruits turn bright colors, the seeds are mature and ready to harvest.

■ To keep ripening seeds from escaping when a pod dries and splits open, slip a net made from an old nylon stocking over the seed head.

Secure it to the stem with a twist tie.

■ Keep dry seeds drier by refrigerating them. This works with both seeds you've collected from dry pods in the garden and leftover packaged seeds. Keeping these seeds in low humidity will encourage a long lifetime. Put collected seeds in dry envelopes. Keep packaged seeds in their original packets as long as they are dry. Enclose them in a sealed plastic bag or glass jar and put them in the refrigerator, where the air is extra arid. Avoid putting them in the humidified produce keepers.

SEEDLINGS INDOORS

■ Instead of buying pots or cell packs, recycle household containers for starting seedlings. Try some of the following:

- Egg crates or milk cartons cut lengthwise

- Clear plastic bakery containers with lids that provide a greenhouselike atmosphere

- Yogurt cups

- Cottage-cheese containers

- Plastic foam coffee cups

Wash the containers thoroughly with soapy water, then sterilize them with a solution of 1 part bleach to 10 parts water. Poke holes in the bottom to allow excess water to drain out.

■ If starting seeds in a window, take extra care to maximize light. Use a south-facing window that will receive sun all day. It should not be blocked by a protruding roof overhang or an evergreen tree or shrub. (Without a south-facing window, it's worth considering building a light garden; see below.)

Hang foil reflectors behind the flat to keep seedlings from leaning toward the sun. If the seedlings are sitting on a windowsill, make a tent of foil behind them, with the shiny side facing the

seedlings. This will reflect sunlight and illuminate the dark side of the seedlings. They will grow much sturdier and straighter as a result. In climates with cloudy weather or homes without south-facing windows, sun may not be reliable enough. A light garden is an ideal solution.

■ For compact, even growth, start seeds indoors under lights rather than in a window. Seedlings must have bright light from the moment they peer up out of the soil.

Set seedlings under a fluorescent shop light. You could place seedlings on a table or counter and suspend the shop light from the ceiling over them. Or you could set up three or four tiered light stands. You can adapt ordinary shelves by attaching lights to the bottoms of the shelves and placing growing trays below each light. Put the lights on a timer set to turn them on for 14 hours a day and off again (one less job for you). You can't beat the results!

■ Make a mini-greenhouse under lights with a clear plastic garment bag. This traps humidity near seedlings, helping to protect them from wilting.

To cover nursery flats full of seedlings, bend two wire coat hangers into arches and prop them in the corners of the flat, one at each end. Work the plastic over the top of the hangers, and tuck the loose ends in below the flat.

It's even easier to make a greenhouse cover for individual pots. Slide two sticks (short bamboo stakes work well) into opposite sides of the pot. Then top with the plastic and fold it under the pot to keep it secure.

■ Start seeds or cuttings in an old aquarium or clear sweater box to keep humidity high. Aquariums or sweater boxes are permanent alternatives to more makeshift options. They are particularly good for cuttings that may need more overhead and rooting room than seedlings. To reuse these containers, wash them with soapy water, rinse, and sterilize with a solution of 1 part bleach to 10 parts water.

SEEDLINGS OUTDOORS

■ Sow perennial and wildflower seeds outdoors in raised beds or spacious nursery pots (the kind you get big flowers in at the nursery) and let nature get them ready to sprout. Hardy perennials and wildflowers often have a special defense called *dormancy* that keeps them from sprouting prematurely during a temporary midwinter thaw (which

would be damaging when the frost returned). They require a certain amount of cold—or alternating freezing and thawing—to indicate when winter is truly over and spring has begun. The easiest way to accommodate the cold requirement is by putting them outdoors.

PLANTS FROM CUTTINGS AND LAYERINGS

Certain plants don't grow from seeds. Named cultivars like "David" phlox must be cloned (vegetatively propagated) to get a plant with all the exact qualities of its parent. This is done by rooting sections of stems or sprouting chunks of roots. Clump-forming plants can be divided into several pieces, and some stems can be rooted while still attached to the mother plant.

CUTTINGS FROM STEMS

■ Be sure to record when you took stem cuttings from roses, lilacs,

Coleus (back) is one of the easiest plants to root from cuttings.

Stems should be strong and moist before they are cut.

geraniums, impatiens, chrysanthemums, dahlias, and other plants. Rooting success often depends on the season in which the cuttings were taken.

■ Take softwood stem cuttings in late spring or early summer for fast rooting. New spring shoots are vigorous but soft and succulent. They may wilt before they root. But if the shoots are allowed to mature for a month or two, they firm up slightly and are ideal for rooting.

■ Take stem cuttings in the morning when they are fresh and full of water. Once the stem is severed from its root, it will not be able to soak up moisture for several weeks or until new roots develop. If

SOME PLANTS SUITABLE FOR SOFTWOOD STEM CUTTINGS

Asters	Bedding geraniums
Bee balm	Lavender
Catmint	Maples
Bellflowers	Mints
Blanketflowers	Phlox
Blueberries	Plumbago
Bugleweed	Russian sage
Chrysanthemums	Serviceberry
Clematis	Tomatoes
Dahlias	Willows
Fuchsias	

These clippings add a touch of beauty to a windowsill, where they can be enjoyed until their roots are long enough for transplanting.

cuttings are started without enough stored moisture, they will simply wilt and die.

■ Use rooting hormone on older or hard-to-root cuttings. Rooting hormones, available in powdered and liquid forms, contain chemicals (called *auxins*) that allow cut stems to begin to produce roots. They must be applied as soon as the cutting is taken and before the cutting is put into sterile planting mix. Not all stems need extra rooting hormone (mints and willows, for instance) as all plants produce some of their own. Adding rooting hormone can make slow starters much more reliable.

■ Avoid feeding softwood shrub cuttings any additional nitrogen after rooting. A little nitrogen, which is available in nutrient-enriched planting mixes, can help the rooting

Take stem cuttings of delphiniums from the base of the plant and not from the flowering stems.

process proceed. But excess nitrogen can encourage fast, tender new growth that is vulnerable to winter damage. Once the cuttings have survived the winter, transplant them into the garden or a larger pot and fertilize them normally.

■ Set a clear glass jar over cuttings of roses, willows, dogwoods, or other easily rooted stems put directly in the garden. The jar will maintain high humidity around the cutting and help prevent wilting. But be sure to protect the jar from the hot sun so the cuttings don't get cooked.

■ Test if a cutting has rooted by gently tugging on the stem. If it shows resistance, roots have formed. After first rooting, allow the roots to develop for several more weeks, if possible, before transplanting.

CUTTINGS FROM ROOTS

Take root cuttings when stem cuttings are not possible. Some perennials, like Oriental poppies and horseradish, have clusters of foliage close to the ground without any stems at all. You can dig up a root and cut it into pieces that may sprout into new plants. With horseradish, you can cut off a side root in the fall and replant it for a new start in the spring. But root cuttings of most other perennials need

more help than horseradish. Here's how to do it:

■ Dig the root in early spring before shoots begin to emerge.

■ Cut the roots into pieces an inch or two long.

■ Lay them horizontally in a flat of well-drained propagating mix such as perlite or coarse sand. Cover lightly.

■ Keep slightly moist but not wet (to prevent root rot) and watch for new sprouts to emerge.

■ When the new plants are growing strongly, transplant them into individual containers or put them out in the garden.

LAYERING

Use layering to propagate hard-to-root shrubs like azaleas. Layering also works well with shrubs that have low-growing or creeping branches, like creeping rosemary. Layered stems develop roots while still connected to the mother plant, which helps encourage the rooting process. Follow these steps:

■ In spring, select a low, flexible branch that will bend down to the ground easily.

■ Prepare well-drained but moisture-retentive soil where the stem will touch the ground.

■ Nick the bark off the side of the stem that will touch the ground and remove the leaves near the nick. Dust the cut with rooting hormone.

■ Cover the barren and nicked stem with soil. Top it with a rock, or pin it in place with a stake or metal pin.

■ The branch tip will become the new plant. If it is an

upright grower, stake the tip upright to give it a good shape.

■ Keep the rooting area moist for several months, until roots develop and become large enough to support the new plant.

■ Cut the new plant free from the parent branch and transplant it to a pot or new site in the garden.

TRANSPLANTING

Whether your new plant is coming from your own seedlings or the garden center, care is needed when it's time to plant it in the garden. Ideally, transplant in the evening or on a cloudy day to keep the sun from causing too much water loss in the plants and burning tender roots or leaves.

■ Don't transplant seedlings into a larger pot until they have one or two sets of true leaves. This allows seedlings to develop enough roots to be self-supporting even if a few roots are lost in the process. It's also a time when seedling

roots are fairly straight and compact, making them easy to separate from nearby plants.

How can you tell when the time is right? It's not as simple as counting the number of leaves on the stem, because the seedling usually has an extra set of leaves called *cotyledons,* or seed leaves. They emerge first and provide food that nourishes the sprouting seedlings. When you look closely, you can see that cotyledons are shaped differently from true leaves. Squash seedlings, for instance, have oval squash-seed–shaped cotyledons that are easy to spot. But the true leaves are broad and lobed.

∎ "Harden off" seedlings and cuttings before they go out into the garden. When growing in the protection of a windowsill, light garden, or greenhouse, young plants are tender and can be easily damaged by strong winds or sun. Toughen them up (a process called *hardening off*) to make the transition from indoors to outdoors successful.

• Days 1 and 2: Put well-watered young plants outdoors in a shady location for several hours. Bring them back indoors when the time is up.

• Days 3 and 4: Increase the length of time seedlings stay outdoors in the shade.

• Days 5 to 7: When well adjusted to shade, gradually move sun-loving plants into brighter light, starting with an hour of sun the first day.

• Day 8 and beyond: When seedlings can stay out all day without burning or wilting, they are ready for transplanting.

Design Details

Growing plants well is a wonderful thing, and arranging them in a handsome landscape is the best way to show them off! A good landscape design plays many roles. It blends the house into the yard, making the entire property look good and increasing property values. Through the design of the landscape, you can create outdoor privacy with vine-covered trellises, hedges, fences, or informal clusters of plants that act like walls of an outdoor room. Knowing the potential of each landscape element allows you to use them for the best effect, making the most of your home and garden.

YOUR LANDSCAPE PLAN

MAPPING THINGS OUT

A simple assessment of your landscape needs is your first step in planning your property. Make a list of the features you want to incorporate into your design. Then you can begin to find the room for it all and start putting the elements in place.

■ Draw a map of your property and decide where the new beds and plantings will go before you start buying and planting. The map needs to be to scale—an exact replica of your property in miniature. Many designers use a scale in which ¼ inch on the plan equals one foot in your yard. This scale usually provides enough room to show

POSSIBLE LANDSCAPE FEATURES

Spatial/Practical:

- Barbecue area
- Children's play areas
- Dog pen and dog run
- Firewood storage
- Lawn for recreation
- Noise reduction
- Party or dance area
- Privacy
- Shade to keep the home cooler
- Sitting/dining areas
- Soil retention for a bank
- Swimming pool
- Wind protection

Aesthetical Considerations:

- Berries for birds
- Eyesore screening
- Floral display
- Hobby gardening (water gardening, herb gardening, etc.)
- Vegetable garden

Flower gardens provide color, beauty, bouquets for the house, and food for birds and butterflies.

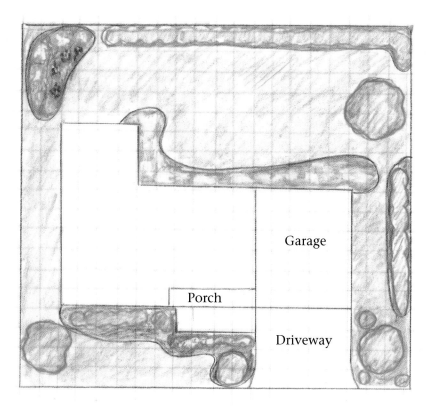

Garage

Porch

Driveway

considerable detail but is likely to require the use of oversized paper so everything will fit on one sheet.

Measure the yard using a measuring tape (50-foot lengths work well), and sketch the perimeter on graph paper. Draw in existing trees, shrubs, fences, and other features you intend to keep, using an overhead view. Make some copies so you can experiment with designs. Then pencil in possible bed outlines and imagine how they will look. Once you've decided on the location of the beds, pencil in the plants you want to add (at the proper spacing) and get an accurate count of how many plants you'll need before you start shelling out any money.

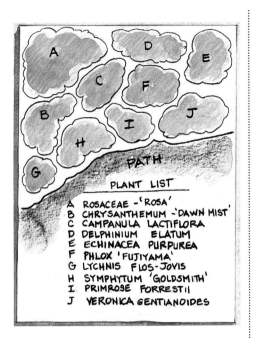

PLANT LIST

A ROSACEAE - 'ROSA'
B CHRYSANTHEMUM - 'DAWN MIST'
C CAMPANULA LACTIFLORA
D DELPHINIUM ELATUM
E ECHINACEA PURPUREA
F PHLOX 'FUJIYAMA'
G LYCHNIS FLOS-JOVIS
H SYMPHYTUM 'GOLDSMITH'
I PRIMROSE FORRESTII
J VERONICA GENTIANOIDES

■ Plan the shape of the lawn, which is usually the biggest feature in a yard. The lawn's shape is more important than the shape of the beds. If it's designed with straight or gradually curving lines, the lawn can make a pretty picture and remain easy to mow. Avoid sharp turns, wiggly edges, and jagged corners, which are irritating to the eye and extra work to mow.

A rounded lawn is pleasing to the eye.

Although the yard may be dormant, you won't forget how it usually looks.

■ Borrow ideas from neighbors' gardens. There is no better way to learn what grows well in your area. You can also get great design ideas from other people. Remember, imitation is the sincerest form of flattery.

■ Take photos and photocopy them. You can shoot the entire front yard or backyard, the plantings around the house's foundation, or individual gardens. Enlarge them on a color copier, if one is available. Then you can sketch in prospective new plants and get an idea of how they will look. Winter is a great time to do this.

■ Visit public gardens and nurseries with display beds for inspiration. These professionally designed gardens may have the newest plants and creative ideas for combining them. Look for gardens about the same size as your yard so you can apply what you learn directly.

BEDS AND BORDERS

▪ Make island beds half as wide as the distance from where you view them. Island beds, often oval or free-form, are situated in areas of lawn where they can be viewed from all sides. They may be near a corner of your yard or by your driveway or entrance walk.

No matter where you put it, an island bed needs to be wide enough to look substantial from your house, patio, or kitchen window— wherever you usually are when you see it. A tiny garden located far from the house is more comical than beautiful. So, for example, if an island bed is 20 feet away, make it 10 feet across. In very large yards, keep beds closer to the house if you don't have time to maintain a large island bed.

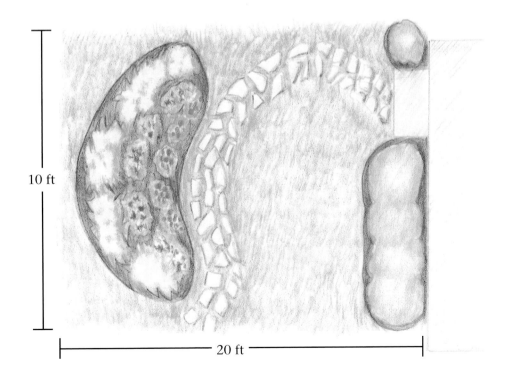

10 ft

20 ft

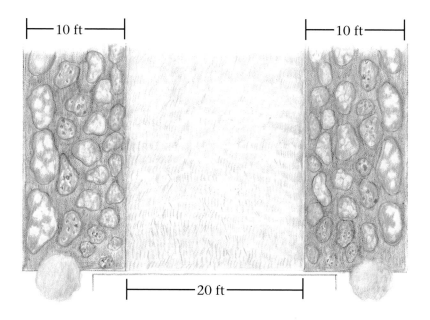

■ Make borders up to half as wide as the total space in a small- or medium-size yard. For example, a 40-foot-wide yard could have one border 20 feet wide or two borders 10 feet wide. Borders—traditional gardens usually set at the edge of a yard, fence, or hedge—also need enough size to be in scale and make an impact in the yard. Wider borders can accommodate taller plants, including trees, shrubs, and large clumps of perennials and ornamental grasses, and so take on a rich diversity.

PATHS AND PAVINGS
Build garden paths anywhere that foot traffic wears out the grass. Paths make pleasing straight or curving lines through the yard and make it easier to get where you need to go in wet weather. They also save you the trouble of having to constantly reseed barren, foot-worn areas.

∎ If you have a large lot, make paths wide enough for two people to walk side by side. If your path is of grass, make it wide enough to accommodate a lawn mower. Give your paths turns or curves so that part of the scene comes as a surprise as you stroll.

∎ Paving materials range in style, price, ease of installation and maintenance, and appearance. Here are four popular options:

• Irregular flagstones create a casual but handsome appearance. The walkway is leveled and laid out more carefully on a gravel bed, with or without mortar. For a more formal appearance, rectangular stones are used.

• Professionally laid brick paving is durable and rather formal. There are several possible patterns and edgings, but simpler styles look best. Paving

bricks are flatter and broader than bricks for buildings. Recycled or antique bricks can be used for pavings and edgings.

• An ordinary concrete sidewalk, plain and simple, is a good-looking and practical choice and is usually less expensive than stone or brick. Be sure to make the path sufficiently broad or it may look too cramped.

• Where a path is needed, and a casual look is desired, wood or bark chips can be used. This kind of path is permeable, so water does not run off, which makes it environmentally friendly. Because the chips break down, a new layer must be added from time to time to refresh the path. The old, decomposing chips can be left in place under the new ones or used for mulching or soil embellishments.

GARDEN ACCENTS

■ Use a collection of pots to end cut-throughs and shortcuts. Gaps in the shrubbery or fencing around your yard are an invitation for neighborhood kids to slip through. Even adults will be tempted to shortcut across the lawn instead of following a longer path up the walk. Reroute traffic by blocking openings and detours with large pots of plants, flowers, herbs, or even your indoor floor plants brought outside in the summer. Cluster them together in a barrier that's not easily skirted. As a bonus, you'll have a dynamic plant grouping with maximum impact on the landscape.

■ Use old concrete from a poured sidewalk as stepping stones in a bed or border. This faux stone is either given away or sold inexpensively by communities conducting sidewalk renovation. Other people may have the same idea, so call well before you need the concrete and get your name on a waiting list if necessary.

■ Create a shade garden without trees by planting under a vine-covered arbor. Shade gardens can feature serene blends of ferns, hostas, and woodland wildflowers, plus a few dazzling bloomers such as azaleas and rhododendrons. Although these plants usually grow amid trees and shrubs, they can thrive in shadows cast by other structures—walls, fences, houses, or a vine-covered arbor.

The advantage of an arbor shade garden is that fewer roots are competing for moisture and nutrients. And unlike a planting close to a wall or building, the arbor shade garden has plenty of fresh air circulation. In addition, an arbor looks great when clad in flowers and handsome foliage.

VINES FOR AN ARBOR

Clematis

Trumpet creeper

Trumpet honeysuckle

Climbing roses

Kiwi vine

Silver-lace vine

American wisteria

Jasmine (warm climate only)

■ Cover rocks and bricks with moss using a buttermilk-moss milk shake. A soft green moss veneer adds an air of antiquity, permanence, and beauty to walls, walks, or woodland rock gardens. You can wait a few years for moss to naturally creep into moist and shady places, or you can encourage a quicker appearance. Gather local cushion-forming mosses, the kinds that thrive in your climate, and find a garden location similar to where they naturally grow. Mix the moss with buttermilk in a blender and pour the concoction onto the appropriate rocks or bricks in your garden. Let it dry thoroughly. Keep the area moist, but not so wet that the milk shake washes off the bricks or stones. New moss will soon make an appearance.

Cover rocks and bricks with a soft carpet of mosslike ground covers or low-growing ground covers.

These midsize bamboo plants are attractive and provide privacy in the yard.

■ Reduce the volume of strong winds by planting a layered assortment of plants as a windbreak. Wind can knock down and dry out plants, generally making it harder to get the garden to grow well. Layered plants—taller trees with shade-tolerant shrubs planted under them—create an irregular barrier that gently stops wind. Solid fences, in contrast, allow wind to slip up and over and swirl back in on the other side.

■ Plant bamboo for a quick and easy screen. Bamboo has handsome foliage and grows in upright thickets that can provide privacy. But most types of bamboo are vigorous spreaders. To keep them from overwhelming a garden, choose clump-forming types or plant them in large,

NOISE REDUCTION

Noise is a nuisance that limits garden enjoyment. Noise from the street or neighborhood is a common offender. Solid walls and dense foliage help block the noise. Berms—mounds of dirt planted with shrubs and perennials—are good for deflecting noise; they also offer a sense of privacy.

submerged tubs or pots that keep the roots contained.

■ Don't forget to place a bench in the garden. You can sit and admire your handiwork, which always looks best up close. Your bench, even a rugged one, can double as garden sculpture.

LAWNS

The emerald green lawn that spreads across most yards serves many purposes: It gives us places to play, filters air pollu-

Attractive seating does double-duty here. It adds interest and charm to the garden while providing a comfortable place to enjoy the view!

Banks of flowers closely line both sides of the path. Note how the grass strips effectively widen the stone path.

tion, cools the air, and softens harsh light. But healthy, beautiful lawns don't just happen; they require work—more than just about any other part of the landscape.

We have become accustomed to fertilizing, spraying, and mowing, mowing, mowing. This kind of pampering can result in a lush and pristine lawn, but it may also be more work than is necessary.

If you're planting a new lawn and want it to be low-maintenance, choose the right kind of grass for the site, plant at the ideal time, and use organic and slow-releasing fertilizers. Or, if you're dealing with an existing lawn, follow our easy hints to minimize maintenance.

■ Use a mixture of turf grasses for a disease-resistant lawn. Diseases that attack one type of grass may not affect the others, so you are reducing the risk of problems.

■ Grass blends also increase versatility. Fine fescues mixed with bluegrass, for instance, are less likely to turn brown in summer heat. Read the labels on lawn grass seed packages closely to identify which grass mixtures are used and how they might affect performance.

■ Plant creeping red fescue in a lightly shaded lawn where bluegrass is likely to fail. For best results, provide well-drained, slightly acidic soil.

■ Consider the merits of sod, seed, and plugs before choosing which to use to start a new lawn:

• Sod: Sheets of prestarted turf can be purchased ready to be laid out on prepared soil, where they will take root and grow. Sod is expensive, but it provides an "instant lawn," and many people like that. It's great on a slope where grass seed can be washed away with the

Public gardens can provide inspiration for your own garden.

first heavy rain. But sod has a few potential problems in addition to its high cost. It may fail to thrive on difficult soils, and your selection can be limited to a few varieties and blends.

• Seed: Grass seed is fairly inexpensive and available in a wide variety of custom mixes; there's something for every kind of lawn. It is best planted in cool, mild weather and must be kept constantly moist to germinate. The grass needs to become well established before summer heat or winter cold push it to the limits.

• Plugs: These are small clumps of sod that can be planted like a ground cover in prepared soil. If kept moist and fertilized, the plugs will spread to form a solid sheet of turf. Plugs are an important way of starting warm-climate lawns and a way to economize in cooler climates.

■ Use seed rather than sod to establish grass on poor soils. Sod roots may never grow into stiff clay soils, which puts a damper on their future if drought strikes. Spend a little extra time and money to improve poor soil with compost. Then plant seed of suitable grasses and tend the lawn well (feeding, watering, raking, and weeding, as necessary) until it is growing strongly.

■ Use edgings to keep grass out of garden beds. A physical barrier can prevent sprigs of grass from spreading to unwanted areas where they can make bed edges look ragged or spring up amid other plants.

Edgings made of 5- to 6-inch-wide strips of fiberglass, metal, or plastic—even stones or brick—can line the perimeter of a garden bed.

Let the upper edge emerge a little above the soil (but well below the level of the mower) and the lower edge sink securely into the ground. More expensive edgings should last longer than cheap plastics, which can shift out of place during winter.

■ Top-dress the lawn with compost or rotted manure to keep it healthy. Unlike super-concentrated fertilizers that stimulate rapid growth, these natural fertilizers provide light doses of nutrients and improve soil conditions. Make sure the compost or manure is finely screened so it will settle down to the soil without packing on top of the turf.

■ Fertilize lawns with slow-release nitrogen fertilizer. Slow-release products gradually emit moderate amounts of nitrogen over a period of weeks or months, so you won't need to fertilize as often. The nitrogen levels in slow-release products are high enough to keep your yard green and healthy, but not so

Longer grass is healthy for the yard—and it means less mowing for you!

high that the lawn is stimulated to grow rapidly and require continual mowing. Read fertilizer bag labels carefully to determine which brands contain slow-release nitrogen.

■ Fill in low spots in uneven lawns by spreading sand evenly over the lawn area with a metal rake. You can sprinkle grass seed on the sand or you can wait for the surrounding grasses to send out new tillers and colonize the fill.

■ Leave grass blades longer for more drought resistance and better root growth. Longer blades shade the soil and roots, keeping them cooler and moister, and the grass roots may grow deeper. In contrast, close-cropped lawns can dry out quickly in summer heat. The stubby blades expose grass-free openings where crabgrass and other weeds can grow.

■ Keep your lawn mower blades sharp. Like a sharp razor on a day-old beard, your mower

Thatch, the dead grass trapped at the soil's surface, needs to be removed periodically.

will slice through grass blades, giving a clean, level cut. Dull blades tear grasses, which can increase their susceptibility to diseases.

■ Dethatch your lawn once a year or as needed to keep it healthy. Thatch is a layer of dead grass stalks that can build up at the soil surface, cutting off air, water, and fertilizer when it becomes thick and matted. Thatch can also harbor pests.

■ A vigorous raking can help break up small amounts of thatch. For big problems, you can rent dethatching machines. Use them in mild

HERBS FOR A FRAGRANT LAWN

Creeping thyme

Roman chamomile

Mint

Clover

Yarrow

Pennyroyal

GRASSES FOR DIFFERENT PURPOSES

Cool Climates: Sun

Kentucky bluegrass

Cool Climates: Sun or Light Shade

Chewings fescue

Creeping red fescue

Moderate Climates: Sun or Light Shade

Hard fescue

Tall fescue

Warm Climates: Sun

Bermuda grass

Zoysia grass

Warm Climates: Sun or Light Shade

St. Augustine grass

Ball Fields

Perennial ryegrass

Golf Courses

Creeping bent grass

weather and plan to reseed if necessary to refill gaps left behind. Once thatch is gone, the clippings can rot to enrich the soil.

■ Don't mow the lawn during drought. Without rainfall, the grass is unlikely to grow much, if at all.

■ Water sparingly during drought. Providing about a half inch of water every two weeks can keep grass alive without encouraging growth.

■ Aerate compacted lawns to keep them healthy. With a lot of foot or wheel traffic, soil can become hard-packed, creating a poor environment for grass

Try planting herbs such as thyme—rather than grass—to create a plush, fragrant lawn.

landscaper or lawn-care company core your yard.

■ Try a fragrant herbal lawn for a change of pace. Herbal lawns release delightful fragrances when you walk on them or mow them. But few herbs will tolerate as much traffic as grass, so it's best to keep them out of the mainstream. You can blend low-growing creeping herbs into grass or plant a smaller area entirely in herbs.

■ Turn a ragged lawn into a meadow by killing the grass and planting perennial wildflowers and grasses. This works best in the privacy of

roots. To help air reach the roots (and also to cut out old thatch), run over the lawn with a core cultivator. This is a machine that pulls up small cylinders of soil, creating breathing spaces. Do-it-yourselfers can buy or rent a core cultivator (see the illustration on page 125). As an alternative, have a

your backyard or in country settings.

■ Consider mowing with a hand-powered reel mower. On a well-tended lawn, reel mowers provide an especially polished cut. They are also quiet and energy efficient.

SELECTING PLANTS

Plant trees and shrubs first, then add flower gardens. Woody plants are the bones of the garden, the bold foundation that will be there summer and winter to enclose your yard or blend your house into the property. They are also the most expensive and permanent features and, as such, need to be given special priority. Plan well, find top-quality trees and shrubs, and plant them properly where they can thrive.

■ Match the flowering plant to the site. Most flowers are high-performance plants, especially sensitive to inadequacies in light, moisture, soil, or other elements. Give them exactly what they need to thrive.

Variation in foliage can provide as much visual interest as flowers.

Experiment with a mixture of warm and cool colors.

■ Select flowering plants with a range of bloom times to keep the garden interesting through the seasons. Many perennials, shrubs, and trees will flower for a maximum of three weeks per year. On paper, list those that bloom in early and late spring, early and late summer, early and late fall. Then when you plant your garden, you can develop a sequence so one kind of flower will fade as another begins to open.

Annual flowers are great for filling the gaps. Pansies, sweet alyssum, and calendula thrive in cool spring and fall weather. Petunias, marigolds, zinnias, geraniums, and other annuals fill the frost-free summer months with color. And tender bulbs such as dahlias and cannas can also provide bright color through much of the warm summer season.

■ Choose flowering plants with good foliage as well as flowers.

The foliage will still be on display long after the flowers are gone. For starters, find plants with foliage that stays healthy, lush, and green and won't become off-colored, ragged, or diseased after flowering. Then you can expand to add plants with golden, silver, bronze, blue, or multicolored leaves that fit the garden color scheme.

■ Use both warm and cool colors to give the garden just the right amount of emphasis. Warm colors such as yellow, orange, and red are bold and visually appear to be closer to you than they are. This makes them ideal for a garden located farther away from your house. Cool colors such as blue and purple recede from the eye and look farther away than they really are. They make pleasant, quiet gardens close to the house, but they may be lost farther away.

PERENNIALS WITH EXCEPTIONALLY LONG BLOOM

Orange coneflowers

Purple coneflowers

Coreopsis

Rose mallow hibiscus

Lenten rose

Violet sage

Sedum 'Autumn Joy'

Asters

'Luxuriant' bleeding heart

Blanketflower

'Stella d'Oro' daylily

Russian sage

Stoke's aster

Pincushion flower

'Sunny Border Blue' veronica

Spiderwort

Mongolian aster

You can blend cool and warm colors to give a feeling of movement and depth in the garden. Color blends also provide vivid contrast, which some people find particularly exhilarating.

■ Consider varying leaf sizes for more design interest. Large leaves like those on hostas or oak leaf hydrangeas advance and stand out (similar to

Use plants with various leaf sizes for visual impact.

SNEAK PREVIEW

If you're designing a flower bed and want the quickest possible preview of your combinations of color and shape, try using the color pictures from last year's seed catalogs to test your ideas. Cut out pictures of plants that interest you. Block out the bed on graph paper and try different pictures in different positions. When you find the combinations that work best for you, use them as a basis for your design.

warm-colored flowers). They are striking in prominent locations, but if overused they will lose their impact.

Small or finely textured leaves, as on thread leaf coreopsis or carrot tops, recede from the eye and look farther away. They can best be appreciated up close. Or if

A weathered wheelbarrow adds a touch of country charm to this garden.

you are trying to make a garden look deeper, these varieties might be used toward the rear as a floral optical illusion. But when used exclusively, fine textured leaves may look busy and weedy.

■ Add the impact of flower size to get another variable for an interesting design. Large flowers are bold and prominent. Smaller flowers and fine flower clusters recede. Blending airy small flower sprays with large, bold flowers combines the best of both textures. Planting larger flowers toward the front of a garden and smaller flowers toward the rear increases visual depth.

Low-Maintenance Gardening

If you are used to cutting your lawn every week and shearing your shrubs once a month, you may be relieved to know that there are easier ways to keep your yard looking nice. Low-maintenance gardening begins with choosing plants ideally suited for your yard's conditions so they won't need coaxing to stay alive.

MINIMIZING UPKEEP

TROUBLE-FREE PLANTING

Some plants are naturally easier to keep, requiring little but suitable soil and proper exposure to grow and prosper. You can plant them and let them be without worrying about pests and diseases or extensive pruning, watering, fertilizing, or staking. Spending a little time finding these easy-care plants will prevent hours of maintenance in coming years.

■ Choose dwarf and slow-growing plants to eliminate the need for pruning and pinching. Tall shrubs just keep growing, and growing, and growing...sometimes getting too big for their place in the landscape. Lilacs, for example, commonly grow to 12 feet high. If planted by the house, they could cut off the

Dwarf shrubs require less pruning than their full-size counterparts.

view from the window. The only solution is regular trimming or replacement. A better option is to grow dwarf shrubs or special compact varieties that will only grow 2 to 4 feet high. They may never need pruning and won't have to be sheared into artificial globes.

COMPACT SHRUBS FOR FOUNDATION PLANTINGS

Dwarf balsam fir

Compact azaleas

Compact barberries

Compact boxwood

Heather

Compact false cypress

Cotoneasters

Daphne

Deutzia

Fothergilla

Hydrangea, French and
  oakleaf

Hypericum

Compact hollies

Compact junipers

Leucothoe

Mahonia

Dwarf Korean lilac

Dwarf spruce

Japanese andromeda

Mugo and other small
  pines

Potentilla

Pyracantha

Roses

Spirea

Stephanandra

Compact viburnums

Tall flowers and vegetables may not be able to support the weight of their flowers and fruit. They might need staking, caging, or support with a wire grid to keep them from falling flat on their faces. Flowers such as delphiniums, asters, and Shasta daisies are now available in compact sizes that are self-supporting. And shorter types of daylilies are less likely to become floppy in light shade than taller types. Compact peas and tomatoes, while not entirely self-supporting, can be allowed to grow loosely on their own, or they may need only small cages or supports to be held securely.

■ Avoid fast-spreading and aggressive perennials such as yarrow, plume poppy, 'Silver King' artemisia, and bee balm. Although these plants are lovely, they have creeping stems that can spread through

Yarrow can spread aggressively if it's not controlled.

the garden, conquering more and more space and arising in the middle of neighboring plants. Keeping them contained in their own place requires dividing—digging up the plants and splitting them into smaller pieces for replanting. This may need to be done as often as once a year. It's better to just avoid them.

■ Avoid delicate plants such as delphiniums, garden phlox, and hollyhocks, which need extra care and staking. Although spectacular in bloom, these prima donnas require constant protection from pests and diseases, plus pampered, rich, moist soil and, often, staking to keep them from falling over. If you simply have to try one, look for compact and/or disease-resistant cultivars, which are easier to care for.

■ Turn a low, moist spot into a bog garden for plants that need extra moisture. You can even excavate down a little to create a natural pond. Plant the moist banks with variegated cattails, sagittaria, bog primroses, marsh marigolds, and other moisture-loving plants. See the list on page 49 for additional plants.

Take advantage of wet soil by planting a bog garden.

CONTAINER GARDENING

Containers are a great option if you're interested in low-maintenance gardening. There is no need to tolerate difficult soil or make do with marginal sites. You can start with any potting mix, picking the perfect blend for the plants you want to grow. You can set the pot where it will have the ideal amount of sun or shade. You provide water when nature comes up short, and you schedule the fertilization. There is nothing left to chance, assuming of course that you take the time to tend the potted plant. In return, containers become living flower arrangements. With lively color schemes, varied textures, and handsome containers, potted plants grow, flower, and flourish close at hand where they are easily enjoyed. Make sure the container is large enough to accommodate the root mass. Undersize containers need constant watering.

Group your pots of annuals together for more visual impact.

■ Plant annuals in a big bag of potting soil for a quick, easy balcony garden. This method, commonly used in England, is still a novelty here and will make a great conversation piece:

• Lay the bag flat on the ground where you want a mini garden. Punch a few small drainage holes in the bottom.

• You can cut one large opening in the top side for several plants, letting them intermingle in a decorative planting scheme. Or make several individual planting holes for a working garden of annual vegetables and herbs.

MATERIALS FOR CONTAINERS

Plastic

Clay

Ceramic

Fiberglass

Brass

Bronze

Tin

Stone

Cement

Cedar

Redwood

Compressed fibers

Compressed peat moss

- The plastic wrapper will help to keep the soil inside moist. But when it does begin to dry out or needs water-soluble fertilizer as a plant pick-me-up, carefully drizzle water or water-soluble fertilizer inside to moisten the entire bag.

■ Use care when planting in decorative containers. Lovely bark, wicker, wood, and even fine pottery and urns make handsome containers. But some of them have one big drawback—they can be damaged by water. Regardless, you can still use them for plants, but only as an ornamental cover over a working pot below. Here is the trick:

- Plant in a plastic pot that has no drainage holes or that sits on a plastic saucer, which will prevent moisture spills.

- The pot, and saucer if used, must be smaller than the decorative container.

- Put a layer of plastic inside the container, then set the potted plant on top.

- Cover the top of the pots with sheet moss or other natural fibers to hide the mechanics below.

A half whiskey barrel is deep and wide and makes a charming container.

This combination will be temporary at best and require careful watering so the plant roots won't be drowned or dried. Once every couple of months, remove the potted plant and water thoroughly, draining off the excess moisture to wash out salts that will build in the soil.

■ Sterilize old pots with a 10 percent bleach solution before using them for other plants. Saving old pots from flowers, vegetables, poinsettias, even shrubs transplanted into the yard is a great way to economize. But you have to be certain to eliminate any pests and diseases that may have come, like extra baggage, with the previous occupant.

Begin by washing out excess soil, bits of roots, and other debris with warm soapy water. Mix 1 part household bleach with 9 parts water and use the solution to wipe out the pot. Rinse again, and the pot is ready to plant.

■ Create your own custom potting soil. Use a peat-moss-based potting mix as the foundation. (It works well for houseplants, seedlings, and many other plants as is.) Peat-based mixes won't compress like true soil, which is a big advantage in pots. But they are low on nutrients and liable to dry out quickly, complications that can be minimized with special potting blends.

• To make a richer mix for annual flowers or for perennials like daylilies, you can blend 2 parts peat mix with 1 part compost.

• For a more fertile, moisture-retentive soil for tomatoes or lettuce, blend 1 part peat mix, 1 part garden soil, and 1 part compost.

• For a lighter mix for propagating cuttings or growing succulents or cacti, add 1 part coarse sand or perlite to 1 part peat mix.

Containers give an extra dose of color and texture to your garden and are a great option in places where the soil is poor.

■ Premix a wheelbarrow full of potting blend. If you have plenty of houseplants that need repotting, or you like to put more than just a few pots or window boxes of summer flowers outdoors, this will save you time and effort. And if you buy the peat mix and extras in large, economy-size bags, it also will save you money.

■ Premoisten peat-based mixes in a large tub or wheelbarrow. Prewetting peat moss, which soaks up a surprisingly large amount of water, ensures there will be enough moisture left over to supply new plantings.

Premoistening is easily done with a garden hose. Sprinkle in a generous amount of water, and work the moisture

into the peat mix with a trowel (or a hoe if you are making large batches). Continue to add more water until the peat clumps together in a moist ball. Then it is ready to go in a pot. Don't let the mix get soggy.

■ Place a circle of fine mesh screen over pot drainage holes instead of using pebbles or pot shards. The screen will help to hold the soil in place until the roots fill out and claim every particle. But it's still a good idea to water outdoors, in the sink, or over a pot saucer so a little oozing dampness or soil won't damage anything.

The problem with covering drainage holes with pot shards (the clay chunks left after a pot is broken) and pebbles is that they can shift to clog up the drainage holes. With no place for excess water to go, plant roots may soak in saturated soil, a condition few plants emerge from alive.

■ Use water-holding gels to reduce the need for watering, especially when planting in quick-drying, peat-based mixes. These gels—actually polymers—look like crystals when dry and safely sealed in their package. But once you add water, you'll be surprised to see them swell into a large mass of quivering gelatin look-alikes. You can blend the gel into potting mixes, following blending instructions on the package.

■ Use window boxes to brighten your house with flowers and add height to surrounding gardens.

• Elegant window boxes can feature flowers that match the color of nearby curtains, carpets, shrubs, or shutters.

• Some cascading ivy, vinca vine, or vining petunias will

Water-holding gels keep the potting mix moister longer than water alone.

soften the geometric outlines of the window box.

• Grow herbs such as thyme, basil, and parsley in a kitchen window box.

■ Set a narrow perforated PVC pipe in the center of a strawberry pot or large container before filling in around it with potting mix. When you need to water your plants, run the hose gently into the pipe, and the water will ooze out from top to bottom, inside to outside, giving every plant an even share.

■ Use slow-release fertilizers to keep plants growing and blooming all season. Because peat-based mixes contain little or no natural nutrients, plant growth depends on a regular supply of fertilizer. Slow-release fertilizers keep working for several months to a year, depending on the formulation.

Keep a watertight saucer, either clay or plastic, under flowerpots.

■ Seal the bottoms of clay saucers with polyurethane to keep them watertight. Then they will be safe to use on floors and carpets. Or, instead of buying clay saucers, you can buy watertight plastic saucers made to look like clay. When one is sitting beneath a pot, it's hard to tell the difference.

FOLIAGE PLANTS FOR CONTAINERS

These plants look great when they're mixed with flowering plants in pots:

- Caladiums
- Crotons
- Elephant ears
- Ferns
- Asparagus ferns
- Coleus
- Rex begonias
- Hostas
- New Zealand flax
- Scented geraniums
- Artemisias
- Spider plants
- Ivies

■ Keep a succession of new flowers blooming in pots throughout the seasons, so your home and yard will never be short on color.

- In spring, enjoy cool-season flowers like forced bulbs, primroses, and pansies.

- In summer, grow tender perennials and annuals like impatiens and begonias.

- In fall, enjoy late bloomers like asters, mums, and ornamental grasses.

■ Put clay and plastic pots in the garage before cold winter weather arrives. This will help keep them from cracking and chipping when the weather turns bitterly cold.

■ Wrap heavy urns and pots that are too bulky to carry indoors in plastic for winter protection. Do this on a dry autumn day, securing the plastic across the top, bottom, and sides of the pots to prevent moisture from getting inside. Moisture expands when it freezes. This causes terra-cotta, ceramic, and even synthetic stone and concrete containers to chip and break.

water reservoir in the bottom that's connected to the pot by a water-absorbing wick. When the soil begins to get dry, the wick pulls up more water from the reservoir.

REDUCING MAINTENANCE

Selecting the right style of planting for any given area can also reduce maintenance. Instead of lawn grass that needs regular fertilizing, watering, and mowing, a self-sustaining meadow area can be appealing and leave you with plenty of time for your other interests. This and other tips will help your landscape look great with less effort.

■ Store pots under a tarp for protection in mild climates. This will save space in your garage or basement and keep the pots handy for when you need them in the spring.

■ Look for self-watering planters if you aren't home enough to keep potted plants from drying out (or if you forget to water every day or two). Self-watering planters have a

■ Plant weedy spots with thick-growing ground cover to avoid becoming a drudge to weeding. Ground cover works well on banks, in sun or shade, under fencing where it's hard to keep weeds down,

Ground cover plants are a low-maintenance option for shady areas where grass won't grow well.

beside outbuildings, and even under trees where it's too shady for grass to grow.

It's important to start the ground-cover bed in weed-free soil, however, so the ground cover can take over without competition. Another option is to clean up the soil. Turn it over with a rototiller or spade, let the weeds sprout, and then turn it again. Repeat the process until the weeds are almost gone.

Choose a ground cover that will thrive on the site. It needs to spread vigorously and grow thickly enough to crowd out any weeds. In shady areas, try pachysandra, barrenwort, or wild ginger. In sun, try creeping junipers, daylilies, ground-cover roses, or other plants that are specifically suited for your climate.

For good results fast, buy plenty of plants and space them relatively close together. If this is too expensive, spread plants farther apart, and mulch the open areas to discourage weeds. Plan to keep a close eye on the new garden for the first year and pull up or hoe down any weeds that appear. Water and

Mix groundcover plants for a tight, weed-proof tapestry of color.

SOME MEADOW PLANTS

Black-eyed Susan

Evening primrose

Coreopsis

Blanketflower

Native grass

Goldenrod

Sunflowers

Aster

Coneflower

Shasta daisy

Snow-in-Summer

Butterfly flower

Maiden pinks

Penstemon

Rock cress

Wild lupine

Gayfeather

fertilize as needed to get the ground-cover plants growing and spreading quickly. Once they've covered the soil solidly, there won't be any space for weeds.

■ In areas distant from the house, plant native meadow grasses and flowers that only need to be mowed once a year. Then have fun watching meadow garden flowers come and go throughout the season.

You can find seed mixes or prestarted turflike carpets of meadow plants specially blended for different regions of the country. To feature your location's unique meadow plants, just let the area grow wild, and meadow plants will come on their own. (Be sure to explain what you are doing to your neighbors so they won't think your lawn mower is broken!)

While they are getting started, newly planted meadows will need weeding and watering. Once in the late fall—after the flowers and grasses have all set seed—mow them down and let the seeds scatter to come up next year. Purchased wildflower carpets and mixes may contain colorful flowers that disappear after several years. You can

A meadow garden of poppies and daisies, though not native, is colorful in early summer.

Wild sunflowers, though not as showy as these hybrids, are beautiful in meadows and gardens.

sprinkle new seeds or plug in new clumps of a wildflower carpet to reintroduce them for color if you want.

■ Mow down old flower stalks in late fall to clean up a flower garden. Before mowing anything but grass with your mower, make sure it has a safety feature that will prevent debris from being thrown out at you. Using suitable lawn mowers can save you plenty of time compared to cutting back the flower stalks by hand. If you allow the old stems to scatter around the garden instead of bagging them, you may find an abundance of self-sown seedlings arising in springtime.

■ Speed up the compost-making process by chopping up leaves and twigs before putting them on the compost pile. The smaller the pieces are, the faster they will decay. Chopping can be easily done with a chipper-shredder or a mulching mower.

Edible Plants

Whether you like to cook or just to eat, nothing tastes as good as something you've grown yourself. Spring is a wonderful time for tender, succulent lettuce, spinach, asparagus, and strawberries. In summer, the bounty includes juicy tomatoes, colorful bell peppers, and sweet blueberries. Squashes, melons, pumpkins, and more salad greens make up the fall harvest.

VEGETABLES

A vegetable garden can be the perfect addition to your landscape. Situate it in a sunny place and start growing food early in the spring. Keep planting all summer long so something fresh and tasty is always ready to harvest.

But fresh and flavorful produce is just the beginning. Growing your own vegetables organically ensures healthful produce and saves you the high

Plant your garden near the house so you'll have easy access to the vegetables.

prices of organically grown produce at the grocery store.

■ Place the garden near your kitchen. It will be easy to run out and pick a few things you need, and you can spy on the garden from your window. Picking tomatoes after you see them blush crimson is a perfect way to get them at their best.

■ Soak seeds to get a jump on the season. Before germinating, seeds need to drink up moisture, just as if drenched by spring rains. Once they become plump and swollen, the little embryo inside will begin to grow.

Seeds such as broccoli, cabbage, and arugula use moisture efficiently and germinate promptly without presoaking. But slower-starting parsley and parsnip seeds benefit from presoaking. Dunk the seeds in room-temperature water for several hours or even overnight, but don't forget them and leave them in too long. Drain and plant the seeds immediately.

■ Use water-filled tepees around early planted tender vegetables for protection from the cold. You can buy inexpensive plastic sheets of connected tubes that, when filled with water, form self-supporting walls around seedlings. The clear walls allow sun to penetrate to the plant inside while the solar-heated water stays warm into the night.

■ Rather than direct sowing, start with large seedlings grown on the windowsill or purchased at a nursery for quick results especially in cold climates. This strategy works well for tender vegetables such as beefsteak tomatoes and chili peppers, which take a long time to ripen but must squeeze in their performance before the last curtain—frost—does them in for the season.

For some vegetables, it's better to plant seedlings.

Look for seedlings grown in large pots (check for a strong, well developed root system) with healthy green leaves and a sturdy constitution. Avoid neglected, spindly, or overgrown seedlings.

Note that not every seedling transplants well when older. Cucumbers, squash, zucchini, pumpkins, and gourds are best started by direct sowing or from young seedlings planted carefully to minimize root disturbance.

■ Plant leggy vegetable seedlings deeper (up to the first set of leaves) to provide a stronger start outdoors. Seedlings started indoors or in crowded greenhouses—places without enough light—may develop lanky, barren stems that topple over in the garden. As long as they grow from a single stem (rather than a rosette of leaves) and go into well-drained soil,

leggy seedlings can be submerged slightly deep for extra support.

For flexible-stemmed seedlings like tomatoes, a horizontal planting trench is better than a vertical one. It is warmer and better aerated than deeper soil, encouraging good root growth and fast development.

■ Keep cutworms away from seedlings with the cardboard centers of toilet paper rolls— recycling at its best! Cutworms, which are moth caterpillars, creep along the soil surface, eating tender stem bases of young seedlings and cutting sprouts off at the roots.

After planting, just set a 3-inch-long cardboard tube around the seedling. Push the tube down so half is submerged, thus preventing underground attacks. Then once the seedling has grown into a plant, you can remove the cardboard collar.

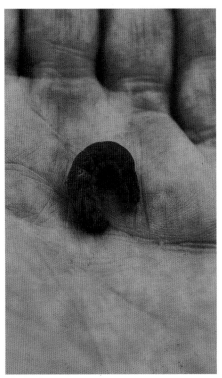

Cutworms are common garden pests.

■ Tear the tops and bottoms off peat pots when setting out vegetables. Peat pots, which are supposed to decay when submerged in the soil, don't always break down the first year they are planted. This leaves plant roots captive inside. To complicate matters further, if the peat rim emerges above the soil surface, it can dry out and

VEGETABLES: FLAVORFUL AND ATTRACTIVE

Experiment with vegetables that are extra pretty or extra flavorful, such as the following:

■ Ruby- and pink-leaved lettuces

■ Green, yellow, and purple snap beans; the purple ones turn green when cooked

■ Crimson, white, gold, and red-striped beets

■ Violet, neon pink, soft pink, and white eggplants

■ Peppers ranging from sweet to mild spicy to super hot—something for everyone

■ Red, orange, yellow, pink, or cream tomatoes; for exceptional flavor, try 'Brandywine' and 'Sweet 100' cherry tomatoes

drying out and gives roots a way to escape if the peat pot persists.

steal moisture from the surrounding soil and nearby roots. Peat pot problems are easily solved by tearing off the top and bottom of the pot before planting. This helps eliminate the danger of

■ Plant vertically to save space. Instead of letting beans, cucumbers, melons, and squash sprawl across the ground, you can let them climb a trellis or arbor.

■ Add height to a vegetable garden with a tepee covered with bean and pea vines. This space saver works similarly to a trellis but has a different

This attractive trellis is a real space saver.

look. Make the tepee of six or eight 6-foot-high poles tied together at the top. Plant pole beans, lima beans, or peas around each pole, and they will twine up to the top.

■ Side-dress long-growing crops, such as indeterminate tomatoes, eggplants, and peppers, with a balanced vegetable-garden fertilizer to keep them producing. After the first harvest, sprinkle some granular fertilizer around the perimeter of the plants, then work it lightly into the soil and water well. The extra nutrients can encourage blossoming of new flowers and development of fruits afterward.

■ Use newspaper covered with straw between garden rows to eliminate weeds and retain moisture. This dynamic duo works more efficiently together than either one alone. At the end of the growing season, rototill the paper and straw into the soil to decay.

■ Plant melons and cucumbers in the compost pile. (They might grow there anyway if you toss old fruits on the pile in the fall.) Warm, moist, nutrient-rich compost seems to bring out the best in melon and cucumber vines.

■ Extend the fall harvest season for crops such as cabbage, brussels sprouts, and broccoli with a warm coat of straw. Although it may never be fashionably chic, straw does trap heat effectively.

Put bales or piles of straw around the plants, leaving the south side open to the warm sun. Thusly treated, these naturally frost-tolerant plants may stay in good condition deep into fall or even into winter in warmer climates.

ASPARAGUS

Once planted, asparagus takes about four years to become established. It grows best in rich soil in full sun. The plants can last dozens of years, and a good asparagus bed is quite a treasure. The spears of established plants are harvested in spring, when they are under a foot tall.

Asparagus grows best in rich soil with full sun.

At least half of the spears are left to grow into fernlike, leafy stems about four feet tall to feed the plants and keep them healthy.

■ Mulch asparagus every spring with several inches of compost or decayed livestock manure. Asparagus, a greedy feeder, will use all the nutrients it can get its roots on and grow that much better for it. By mulching in the spring, you can fertilize, help keep the soil moist, and reduce weed seed germination all in one effort. The shoots that arise through the mulch will grow especially plump and succulent.

■ Make fancy white asparagus spears with a simple blanching basket. This European connoisseur's vegetable is easy to grow at home. When the spears first emerge in spring, cover them with a bucket, basket, or mound of soil that will exclude all light. Harvest when the spears reach 8 to 10 inches tall and before the ferny leaves begin to emerge.

trellises as well as dwarf forms that squeeze into containers and tight spaces. Pumpkins take lots more space and a longer growing season, so they may not work as well for some gardeners. None of these plants tolerates frost.

BEANS

Beans do not tolerate frost. If you choose climbing types, you can train them upward on tepees and pergolas for nice garden accents. Scarlet runner beans have great flowers and edible beans, and string beans and limas are favorites everywhere.

CUCUMBERS AND SQUASH

You'll find vining or climbing types for

Nothing tastes better than a cucumber fresh from the vine!

If you're short on space, mix edible plants with ornamental ones for a beautiful "Garden of Eden" effect.

EGGPLANTS

With their purple flowers and colorful fruits, eggplants look good in any garden. There are purple, white, streaked, or even red fruits with elongated or globular forms. Eggplants exhibit preferences similar to peppers.

LETTUCE

Lettuce grows during cool weather in spring or fall. Even when crowded, it will produce usable leaves, but plants grow better when widely spaced. In flower beds, an edging or clump of lettuce does double duty. Leaves can be green or red, frilled or plain, depending on the cultivar.

■ Produce late fall, winter, and early spring lettuce by growing extra-hardy varieties such as 'Arctic King' or 'North Pole' and creating sheltered planting places for them:

- Raised beds covered with heavy-duty floating row covers can provide protection from frosts and light freezes in early to mid-spring and mid- to late fall, or even winter in mild climates.

- Cold frames, heated by the sun, make it possible to grow lettuce earlier in spring and later in fall or winter. Cold frames are translucent rectangular boxes, about 2 feet wide, 4 feet long, and 18 inches high. The top is hinged to open so you can tend plants inside or cool the cold frame on mild, sunny days. Plant seeds or seedlings of lettuce in the frame and close the lid to hold in the heat.

- A hot bed, which is a souped-up cold frame, is a great place for winter lettuce. Lay a heating cable

under the cold frame. Cover with wire mesh to prevent damage to the cable and top with a layer of sand mixed with compost.

■ For an extended lettuce harvest, pick the largest leaves from the outside of the plant and allow the younger inner leaves to continue growing. But when springtime weather begins to get warm, you need to take the opposite strategy. Cut off the entire plant before it begins to send up a flower stem (a condition called *bolting*) and turns bitter.

■ Get twice the harvest by planting a lettuce and tomato garden in an 18- or 24-inch-wide pot. You can pick the lettuce as it swells and leave extra growing room for the tomatoes. Here's how to proceed:

• Fill the pot with a premoistened blend of ⅓ compost and ⅔ peat-based potting mix.

• Plant several leaf lettuce seeds or small seedlings around the edge of the pot and a tomato seedling in the middle.

• Place the pot in a sunny, frost-free location.

Peppers range from sweet to mildly spicy to super hot—something for everyone's taste buds!

- Water as needed to keep the soil moist, and fertilize once a month or as needed to encourage good growth.

PEPPERS

Colorful ornamental peppers last longer than flowers and add festive color and texture to beds and borders. Plants range from six inches to several feet tall. Foliage may be green or purple.

The glossy fruits grow from an inch or less in length to more than six inches and can be pointy, round, or blocky. They have bright colors and waxy coats and range from cream through yellow, orange, red, purple, and brownish-black. Grow peppers during warm weather in full sun, after the danger of frost has passed.

TOMATOES

There is nothing like a fresh, sun-warmed tomato, so they are on everyone's list. There are many kinds to consider, from beefsteak to cherry to heirloom varieties. There are also petite types bred specifically for hanging baskets. Tall and rangy cherry types can be trained up a trellis or over an arch.

■ Prune tomato plants to direct maximum energy into tomato production. Choose your pruning plan based on what you want from your tomatoes. For larger and earlier (but fewer) tomatoes, remove any shoots that emerge on or beside the main stem, and tie the stem to a stake. For more tomatoes later, let plants bush out and support them in tomato cages. Pinch off any flowers that open before July 4.

■ Choose between determinate and indeterminate tomatoes

'Better Boy' tomatoes

EARLY, MIDSEASON, AND LATE TOMATOES

Early

'Early Girl'

'Early Pick'

'First Lady'

'Glacier'

'Oregon Spring'

Midseason

'Better Boy'

'Big Beef'

'Big Boy'

'Big Girl'

'Celebrity'

'Delicious'

'Floramerica'

'Heatwave'

Late

'Homestead'

'Oxheart'

'Wonderboy'

'Supersteak'

'Beefmaster'

'Brandywine'

according to the way you prefer to harvest.

Determinate tomatoes (such as 'Celebrity') tend to stay compact and produce most of their tomatoes at about the same time. This is convenient for freezing, canning, and sauce making.

Indeterminate tomatoes (such as 'Big Beef') keep growing and developing new

Small fruits like blueberries and raspberries fit into smaller gardens.

tomatoes as they go. They produce a greater yield but spread it over a longer harvest period.

Dozens of different cultivars are in each class—plenty to pick from. You might have to check seed catalogs to find out whether a particular tomato is determinate or not.

■ Stake your tomato cages so a bumper crop won't pull them over. Work a tall stake through the wire mesh near the perimeter of the cage, and stab or pound it to 8 inches deep in the ground. This will anchor the cage (and the plant inside) firmly despite the pull of strong winds and branchfuls of ripening tomatoes.

FRUITS

So many different kinds of fruit are available—how do you begin to decide which to grow? Start with quality. When soft berries are homegrown, they can be harvested when fully ripe, plump, and sweet, without concern for shipping and perishability. The flavor is out-standing!

The amount of garden space available will be another deciding factor. Choose between growing small fruits—berries that grow on small plants, vines, or bushes—or larger tree fruits. Start with easily raised, space-efficient small fruits such as strawberries, blackberries, and raspberries. But if you have a place in your landscape for a fruit tree or two, don't pass up the opportunity. Look for easy-care fruit trees or even non-traditional trees such as mulberries or crab apples.

FRUITS THAT GROW ON TREES

Traditional orchard trees such as apples, peaches, pears, and

If you have room, tree-ripened pears and other fruits are worth the effort.

cherries require some knowledge and attention to pollination, pruning, pest control, fertilizing, and other kinds of care. To minimize or eliminate spraying for disease, look for new disease-resistant cultivars of apple trees.

■ Plant dwarf fruit trees, which stay small enough for you to pick the fruit from the ground. This is a safe, easy way to harvest. You won't have to lug around ladders or balance on them while working. Another advantage of dwarf fruit trees is they begin to bear fruit much younger than full-size trees do. And if your lawn is small, a dwarf tree, which takes up less space than its full-size counterpart, is a good alternative.

Dwarf fruit trees are a practical choice for small lawns.

■ Try growing a super-dwarf peach tree in a pot. Super-dwarfs are extra-miniature trees that may reach only about 5 feet tall. Although other fruit trees come as super-dwarfs, peaches produce flavorful fruit with only one tree and are great for beginners. (Many other fruit trees require a second cultivar for pollination.)

Plant your super-dwarf peach tree in a 24-inch-wide tub with drainage holes in the bottom. Keep it moist, well fertilized, and in a sunny location during the growing season. If your tree doesn't bear fruit the first year, give it time. It may need another year or two to start its career. During winter in cold climates, store the tree, tub and all, in a cool but protected location.

■ Use sticky red balls that resemble apples for control of apple maggots on apple and plum trees. Apple maggots are fly larvae that tunnel into

Not all insects are pests. Do your homework before you spray.

developing fruit, making it disgusting and inedible.

Apple maggot flies are easily tricked, however. If you put out sticky red balls that resemble apples (homemade or purchased through a garden supply catalog), the egg-laying females will be attracted to the ball and get stuck. (This will end their egg-laying career!) Hang at least one sticky red ball in a dwarf tree and six or more in larger trees.

■ Use tree bands to catch crawling pests climbing up fruit tree trunks. Sticky plastic bands will catch ants carrying aphids and creeping caterpillars such as gypsy moths and codling moths.

RASPBERRIES AND BLACKBERRIES

These fruits grow on thorny canes, which are elongated, semiwoody flowering stems about five or six feet tall. They spread with underground runners and can be aggressive unless severely checked. But they are worth the trouble for the absolutely delicious berries, which can be eaten—still warm from the sun—right off the plants in summer. You may have to cover the ripening berries with netting to protect your crop from the birds.

Fruit breeders have given us types of raspberries that are everbearing or repeat bearing, instead of bearing fruit just once a summer. Most raspberries grow in Zones 4–8.

Blackberries, too, have been worked on by breeders, and you can purchase thornless types that are delicious and have very large berries. Some of these prefer to have their canes staked to poles or other supports. They are self-pollinating and easy to grow, performing best in well-drained soil in Zones 5–8.

Cover your berries with netting to protect them from hungry birds.

■ Cut the canes on blackberries and raspberries when first setting out new plants. The canes are the elongated flowering stems. Leave just a few of the leafy buds at the base of the stems. This eliminates any cane diseases that may have hitchhiked to your garden on the plant. It also discourages spring flowering, letting the plant become well established before moving on to berry production.

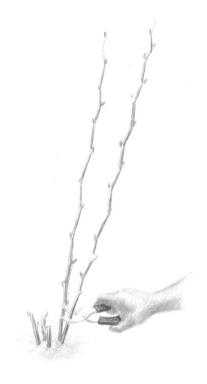

■ Thin out one-third of all blackberry and raspberry canes each year to keep them productive. If you've ever tried to walk through an abandoned farm field bristling with blackberry thickets, you know what a thorny tangle these plants can grow into.

Not only does crowded growth make blackberries and raspberries hard to work around, it also forces the canes to compete for sun, nutrients, moisture, and fresh air. The result can be smaller berries and more diseases.

As soon as canes are done bearing fruit, you can cut them off at the base to provide more space for new canes. Remove any sick, weak, or scrawny canes. Then selectively remove additional canes from areas that are crowded to keep them from creeping into other parts of the garden.

Pruning is easier if you wear thick, thornproof gloves and use long-handled pruning loppers. A pair of sunglasses to protect your eyes won't hurt either.

STRAWBERRIES

Strawberries are fun to have around for garden tastes, even if the crop is not that large.

Various raiders such as birds and squirrels will get most of the crop if you don't keep them out with netting or repellents. The plants like full sun or bright partial shade and moist, rich soil. Buy your plants from local sources for types that thrive in your climate.

Mulch strawberries with straw to keep the fruit clean. Straw keeps soil and disease spores, which cause berries to

Straw helps berries stay healthy and attractive.

neutrals can keep flowering and fruiting throughout much of the summer.

Plant day-neutral strawberries as early in spring as possible and pinch off all the flower buds for six weeks afterward. This lets the plants grow strong before they begin to fruit. Once the plants are flowering, fertilize them monthly to keep the plants vigorous and productive.

rot and mold, from splashing up onto the berries. As a result, they look nicer and keep longer. Straw also keeps the soil moist, so the berries can plump up, and it helps reduce weeds.

■ Grow day-neutral strawberries for a summerlong harvest. While June-bearing strawberries bear fruit heavily in early summer, and ever-bearing strawberries bear in June and again in fall, day-

DISEASE-RESISTANT STRAWBERRIES

'Allstar'

'Cavendish'

'Delite'

'Guardian'

'Lateglow'

'Redchief'

'Scott'

'Surecrop'

Heavy producers such as these may not keep up the pace year after year. When you notice berry production diminishing, consider starting a new strawberry patch with fresh plants.

■ Plant strawberries in a strawberry jar for a delicious feast on a patio. Strawberry jars stand about two feet high and have openings along the side, perfect for planting with strawberry plants. They look especially charming when little plantlets sprout on runners and dangle down the sides.

HERBS

Herbs are useful for cooking, crafting, and decorating—boldly coming out of the garden and into your home. A separate herb garden is wonderful, but herbs can also be blended with flowers

If you don't have the space for a separate herb garden, consider growing a selection of herbs in a container.

An herbal knot garden

You can also grow gourmet varieties of these classics— lemon thyme, cinnamon basil, and Sicilian oregano, for example—to add to your cooking pleasure.

■ Plan an herb garden before you plant. Some of the most charming herb gardens have formal beds or geometric patterns that show off the beauty of herbal foliage. Here are some examples:

• Knot gardens interweave herbs with contrasting leaf color and textures into simple or intricate patterns, many of which are taken from embroidery schemes. Simple knot gardens can be made with two overlapping circles or squares set on a back-ground of mulch or gravel. An easy way to make a knot is with annual herbs

and vegetables in a kitchen or a cottage garden. You can also slip herbs in flower or shrub beds, or even into the plantings around your foundation.

Culinary herbs are a main-stay of most herb gardens. The garden-fresh flavors of thyme, basil, savory, oregano, and marjoram are incomparable.

such as bush basil, summer savory, or sweet marjoram, or even annual flowers such as French marigolds or ageratum.

• Formal herb gardens generally have symmetrical planting plans, with matched herbs on either side of the garden like reflections in a mirror.

• Formal and patterned herb gardens often include neat, clipped edgings of boxwood, teucrium, santolina, thyme, winter savory, or other neat herbs suitable for shearing.

■ Provide sandy soil for herbs that need well-drained soil of moderate fertility. If kept in soil that's lean and light and drenched in hot sun, these herbs develop excellent flavor.

If your soil is naturally sandy and well drained,

This intricate knot garden combines fragrant herbs and shrubs.

you're in luck. If, instead, it's damp clay, raise the herb garden and add a 3-inch layer of coarse sand and 2 inches of compost to improve drainage. Avoid excessive use of fertilizers, especially those high in nitrogen.

■ Grow herbs that need light soil in pots. When planted in well-drained, peat-based potting mix, herbs such as thyme, lavender, and rosemary thrive—and they look great!

■ Plant perennials that double as herbs in flower beds and borders. Some herbs masquerade as perennials (and vice versa) because they can be used for decorating, fragrance, or cuisine. Some examples include the following:

- Sweetly fragrant bee balm has flowers and foliage wonderful for tea or drying for potpourri.

- Yarrow bears everlasting flowers for dried floral arrangements. Air drying is fine for golden-flowered forms. To preserve the color of pink, red, and white-flowered yarrows, dry them in silica gel.

- Lady's mantle is a historical herb with lovely scalloped leaves and small sprays of yellow-green flowers for cutting.

- Pinks have fragrant flowers that can be used fresh for cut-flower arrangements or dried for potpourri.

■ Use herbs with attractive foliage for season-long color

Thyme is a versatile, free-blooming plant for herb gardens and borders alike.

Lavender's fragrant flowers can be dried for potpourri.

in perennial gardens. Amid the comings and goings of perennial flowers, neatly or colorfully clad herbs maintain enduring style and beauty.

■ Some of the best herbs to grow for decorative foliage include globe basil (small mounds of emerald green), bronze leaf basil or perilla, ornamental sages (with purple leaves, variegated gold leaves, or tricolor green, white, and pink leaves), and silver-leaved herbs such as gray santolina and lavender.

For a great overall color scheme, complement the color of the foliage with nearby flowers.

■ Plant a collection of commonly used culinary herbs in a clay planter by a sunny kitchen window. They will be right at hand when you need them.

■ Restrain rampant herbs like mint and bee balm so they can't take over the garden. These plants need firm limits to keep them in their proper place.

Plant rampant herbs in large plastic pots with the bottom removed and the top rim emerging an inch or two above the soil surface. The container will slow down

SOME HERBS FOR MOISTER SOIL

Angelica

Basil

Bee balm

Chives

Horseradish

Lady's mantle

Lemon balm

Mints

Parsley

Sorrel

Sweet woodruff

spreading growth enough so you can see trouble before it spills over the edge. Cut back any errant sprouts and use them for tea or to garnish a fruit salad. Divide to renew the chastised plant every year or two.

■ Pinch back annual herbs, such as basil, to keep them from blooming. If allowed to channel energy into seed production, the foliage will grow skimpy and so will your

SOME HERBS FOR LIGHT SOIL

Lavender

Sage

Santolina

Thyme

Oregano

Sweet fennel

Marjoram

Winter savory

Yarrow

Lamb's ears

Teucrium

German chamomile

Coriander

Sweet fennel

Sage

Hyssop

Tarragon

Rosemary

Artemisias

harvest. Pinching off the shoot tips from time to time provides sprigs for herbal vinegars and pestos and inspires the plant to grow back bushier than ever.

■ Remove a few bricks in a garden path to make places for low-growing thyme or oregano. Either herb will thrive in this warm, well-drained location and will give a charming natural look and wonderful fragrance to the walkway.

■ Plant more parsley, dill, and fennel than you think you will use to attract swallowtail butterflies. The beauty of the butterflies and fun of watching the caterpillars develop can be worth the foliage they eat.

■ Harvest perennial herbs as they develop flower buds. This is the time when the fragrant and flavorful oils in the plants are at their peak of intensity, providing a gourmet experience. Because

Black swallowtail butterflies nectar on a variety of plants like this verbena, but larvae eat only umbells like dill.

fresh herbs taste so good, even at other times of the growing season, it's perfectly acceptable to continue harvesting whenever you feel the urge. In cold climates, however, hardy perennial herbs need a break from heavy harvesting beginning 45 days before the first frost in order to prepare for winter.

Annuals and Biennials

Annuals are flowers that bloom the first year they are planted, often flowering just a couple of months after sowing. Most annuals are started indoors or in greenhouses in late winter or early spring. Biennials like cup and saucer, some foxgloves, and some hollyhocks produce only greenery the first year. During the second year of growth, they flower and set seed destined to become the next generation. If you allow plants to self-sow for at least two years, you will have a steady supply of blooming plants.

WHAT IS AN ANNUAL?

TENDER ANNUALS

Some annuals, called *tender annuals,* are killed by frost. They grow in hot weather and are started indoors or in greenhouses and then set out in the garden after the danger of frost passes. Some of the faster-growing tender annuals, such as zinnias and marigolds, can be sown directly into garden beds—after the frost in spring—for bloom or use all summer long. This depends on many factors, including where you live and how long summer weather lasts.

Black-eyed Susans produce a wealth of summer flowers and will freely reseed themselves.

ANNUALS IN WARM CLIMATES

Gardeners who live in warm climates with little frost (mainly Zones 9 to 11) can do really interesting things with annuals and grow them throughout the year, using tender annuals and tender perennials in spring, summer, and fall.

In winter, hardy annuals can be put to great use. Plant seeds of shirley poppies, larkspur, pansies and violas, baby's breath, cornflowers, sweet peas, and other hardy annuals directly in the sunny garden in November and December, after the weather cools. Thin the seedlings if they are too crowded. They'll grow through the shifts of cool and warm weather of the South's winter. A few months later, fabulously colorful blooms will be delightful.

HARDY ANNUALS

These annuals have some built-in frost tolerance. They are often, but not always, planted outside from seed a few weeks before the final frost, but sometimes they are started indoors in warmer conditions, hardened off for a good adjustment, and planted outside during spring (or in winter in Zones 8 to 10).

BIENNIALS

Sown in summer or fall, biennials, such as sweet william, develop their roots and foliage and live through the winter. Then they come quickly into a spectacular but short-lived period of bloom in spring. They tend to self-sow, providing a constant supply of plants. Hardy annuals grow like biennials where winters are not too cold.

TENDER PERENNIALS

This grouping includes other plants that are mainly used as annuals. In colder climates, tender perennials, such as wax begonia and some species of impatiens, will behave like annuals and must be cultivated as such. These same plants will grow as perennials in their native, hot climates, living for several years.

This rock-lined annual border of pansies and snapdragons is perky and colorful for weeks on end.

DESIGNING WITH ANNUALS

COLOR

Designing with annuals gives lots of importance to flower color. Annuals offer flower color for a longer period of time than other plant types, for they are constantly in bloom. They are often used in complex plans.

Flowers are not the only source of color in annual gardens. Many plants, such as the dramatic purple orach and more muted silver-gray dusty miller, are treasured for their foliage alone. Others (such as cockscombs) have both colorful foliage and flowers. And still others—ornamental peppers, eggplants, and dolichos, for instance—provide garden color with their attractive fruits.

■ Use pale sand to outline the plant groupings on the well-prepared soil before planting

Dusty miller is prized for its beautiful gray foliage.

when laying out annual beds. This is like making a pencil sketch of a painting before stroking on the oil paints.

Whether you're planning to put blue ageratums in edging rows, make a teardrop of red zinnias, or create a sweeping mass of pink impatiens, you can adjust and fine-tune the overall shapes before filling them in with colorful flowers. After making the sand outlines, stand back and look at the results objectively. If you don't like the first attempt, cover the sand with soil and try again.

■ Re-create a favorite pattern from a family crest, piece of fabric, or needlepoint with annuals in your flower garden. You've seen similar patterns at amusement parks and public gardens. Why not do the same with a pattern that is meaningful to you?

■ For something simple and different, consider the massed approach: Select one favorite, and flood the entire planting area with it. This approach eliminates deciding where to plant a particular variety, selecting which colors and textures blend together well, or learning the cultural requirements for more than one kind of plant. The entire bed can be prepared and planted in a day.

Gardens don't have to be rectangular—use your imagination to come up with a creative pattern.

TEXTURE

Another decorative aspect of plants is their texture or surface. Compare the large, coarse texture of the sunflower to the fine, soft bachelor's button. Fill masses with fine-textured plants, and reserve heavier-textured annuals for contrast or accent. Most often, we think of foliage as the sole textural source, when texture can be added equally often by flowers.

FORM

Consider the overall growth habit of each annual plant. Flower forms include tall spikes, round globes, sprays, and clusters. Plant forms range from tall and skinny to low and ranging. Try interplanting tall, open annuals with a spreading carpet of contrasting form. A garden is more visually stimulating when a variety of forms is used.

Bold sunflowers look great planted in masses. The faces follow the sun throughout the day.

Because of its height, cosmos should be planted at the back of borders.

SCALE

When planning your annual garden, it's important to keep in mind scale (the size of the plant). Miniature plants are great to use in small spaces and where people are close enough to see them, but in a large area, they can become completely lost. On the other hand, large-growing plants such as spider plants, cosmos, and nastur-tiums may dominate and even smother out smaller neighbors when space is limited. In general, plant tall, spikelike annuals in the background of mixed beds, while reserving closer foreground seats for smaller, delicate beauties.

Plant staggered rows of annuals to create a fuller look. A single marching line of annuals such as French marigolds set

Bright-colored impatiens are good flowers to have in a shade garden.

side by side can look weak in a bigger garden. You can beef up their impact by planting a second row behind the first, with the rear plants centered on the openings between the front-row plants.

Staggered rows are also nice for showcasing taller annuals, such as blue salvia or snapdragons, set in the rear of a garden. A double row of spider plants can become so full and bushy it resembles a flowering hedge.

ANNUALS IN THE SHADE

■ Choose shade-tolerant or shade-loving annuals for a lightly shaded garden. Among the annuals that prefer shade are impatiens, browallia, and torenia. Other annuals, the most versatile of the bunch, will grow in sun or light shade. They include wax begonias, sweet alyssum, ageratum, coleus, forget-me-nots, and pansies.

■ Create the most excitement from your shade garden by choosing flowers with white, pastel, or brightly colored blossoms. Dark burgundy leaves and cool blue or purple flowers won't shine the way brighter blooms do from shady garden depths.

OTHER WAYS TO USE ANNUALS

Since annuals are plants that grow fast, they have many practical uses in and out of the garden.

■ Use annuals to fill gardens that will later be used for perennial borders when the budget permits or the plants have multiplied enough to fill the space. Because annuals stay in bloom for several months at a time, they are used for constancy in gardens where other plants come in and go out of bloom.

This hot color combination features annuals, biennials, and perennials.

Globe amaranth can be dried for use in winter arrangements.

■ Grow some annuals with everlasting flowers to dry for winter arrangements. There are many wonderful annuals to choose from. Those listed at right are easily dried if spread out in a warm, dark, airy place. Grow a few for yourself and some extras to give away as gifts.

If seedlings of everlasting annuals are not available at your local garden center, consider starting your own seedlings indoors.

SOME EVERLASTING ANNUALS

Cockscomb: plume or comb-shape flowers in bright red, orange, or yellow

Annual baby's breath: cloudlike drifts of small white flowers

Bells of Ireland: spikes of green trumpet-shape flowers

Globe amaranth: ball-shape flowers of white, pink, purple, and orange

Love-in-a-mist: maroon-striped seedpods

Statice: bright sprays of pink, purple, yellow, white, and blue flowers

Strawflowers: double daisylike flowers with straw-textured petals in red, pink, white, gold, and bronze

■ Relive a little slice of history by growing a few heirloom flowers. These are flowers your ancestors may have enjoyed. Many of these plants are returning to popularity, thanks to their interesting appearances. Some heirlooms are only slightly different from modern flowers—taller, larger- or smaller-flowered, or more fragrant. But other heirlooms are quite distinct and unusual. Here are some examples:

Staking sweet peas to the house adds a lovely, old-fashioned touch to the garden.

• Love-lies-bleeding: Long, dangling, crimson red seed heads form colorful streamers.

• Kiss-me-over-the-garden-gate: These six-foot-tall plants have pendulous pink flowers.

• Balsam: This impatiens relative sprinkles flowers amid the foliage along the stems.

• Sweet peas: Vining pea-shape plants that bear

colorful pink, white, purple, and red flowers with delightful fragrances.

CARE AND FEEDING

PLANTING

■ Choose healthy plants when shopping at the garden center or nursery in spring. Here is a checklist to use before buying any new plant:

•Leaf color: The foliage of naturally green-leafed

ANNUALS SUITABLE FOR LATE-SUMMER CUTTINGS

- ■ Geraniums, ivy-leaf and standard
- ■ Impatiens
- ■ Fibrous-rooted begonias
- ■ Coleus
- ■ Asters
- ■ Portulaca
- ■ Verbena

plants should be bright green, not faded yellow or scorched bronze or brown.

- Plant shape: The sturdiest seedlings will be compact, with short stretches of stem between sets of leaves. A lanky, skinny seedling is weaker and less desirable than a short, stocky one.

- Pests: If you shake the plant, no insects should come fluttering off. Inspect the stem tips and flower buds for aphids, small pear-shape sap suckers. Look for hidden pests by turning the plant upside down and looking under the leaves and along the stem.

- Roots: An annual with ideal roots will have filled out its potting soil without growing cramped. When roots are overcrowded, the plant is root-bound—the roots have consumed all soil space and grown tangled. The best way to judge root quality is to pop a plant out of its container

(or ask a salesclerk to do this) and check to see how matted the roots have become.

■ Gently break up the root-ball of annuals grown in cell packs or pots before planting them. Often, the roots have overgrown the potting area and become matted. You'll have to pull off the tangles so the roots will be able to grow freely into the soil.

If roots are wound around the bottom of the root-ball, use your finger to gently work

ANNUALS FOR CONTAINERS

■ Fibrous-rooted begonia
■ Petunias
■ Calendula
■ Coleus
■ Dracaena
■ Impatiens
■ Lobelia
■ Marigold
■ Nasturtium
■ Ornamental pepper
■ Pansy
■ Perilla
■ Phlox *(P. Drummondii)*
■ Sweet pea
■ Verbena
■ Viola
■ Zonal geranium

the roots free of each other. If they are matted over the entire root-ball, you'll need to tear or cut the mats off, leaving the roots below intact.

■ Use a spacing aid to plant annual displays and cutting gardens in even rows. Even the most beautifully grown annuals can be distracting if they are spaced erratically. Fortunately, spacing is one element you can easily control. Here are some options:

• Make a planting grid by stapling a large piece of wire mesh over a wooden frame. If the mesh

FRAGRANT ANNUALS

Why not plant some perfumed flowers under an open window or beside the patio? Here are some good choices:

■ Pinks

■ Heliotropes

■ Petunias

■ Moonflowers

■ Lemon and Orange Gem marigolds

■ Fragrant white flowering tobacco

■ Stocks

■ Sweet peas

openings are 2 inches square and you want to plant ageratums 6 inches apart, you can put one seedling in every third hole.

- Make a spacing rope. Tie knots in the rope to mark specific measurements, for instance, noting every 4 or 6 inches. You can stretch the rope between two stakes to make even measurements along a straight line.

- Take a yardstick with you when you go to plant. Measure the distance between each plant in a row and between rows rather than simply eyeballing it.

KEEPING THINGS TIDY

■ Snip back leggy annuals when you plant to encourage bushy new growth. Don't hesitate—it's really for the best! Removing the growing tip of a stem stimulates side shoots to sprout, which makes annuals fuller. Since each side shoot can be full of flowers, the whole plant will look better.

■ Remove spent blossoms from geraniums and other annuals to keep them blooming and tidy. The bigger the flower, the worse it can look when faded, brown, and mushy. Large, globular geranium flowers are particularly prominent when they begin to discolor. Snip off the entire flower cluster. Take off the bloom stalk, too, if no other flower buds are waiting to bloom.

This process, called *deadheading,* is more than mere housekeeping. By removing the old flowers, you prevent seed production, which consumes a huge amount of energy from the plant. Energy saved can be channeled instead into producing new blooms.

■ Pinch annuals like coleus, browallia, and petunias to keep them full. These plants can get tall and gangly as the growing season progresses. A little pinch, removing the top

Keep geraniums tidy and producing by removing the old flowers.

inch or two of stem, will soon correct this problem.

More is at work here than merely shortening the stem. Removing the terminal bud (at the stem tip) allows side branches to grow and make the plant fuller.

FERTILIZING

Fertilize annuals periodically during the growing season to keep them producing. This is particularly helpful after the first flush of blooming flowers begins to fade (which often marks the beginning of a quiet garden during hot summer months).

For best results, dead-head, then fertilize with a balanced water-soluble or granular fertilizer. A balanced fertilizer contains similar percentages of nitrogen, phosphorus, and potassium. Check the fertilizer package label for application instructions. In containers, use a slow-release fertilizer that releases nutrients every time you water.

Some petunias are self-branching. They stay fuller naturally and may not need any pinching.

INCREASING ANNUALS

Take stem cuttings of tender flowers in late summer before temperatures drop below 50 degrees Fahrenheit. You can root them indoors and enjoy their greenery and perhaps a few flowers during winter. Then you can take more cuttings of these plants to set out next spring. Cuttings are more compact and versatile than old garden plants dug up and squeezed into a pot. They can thrive with less effort and space.

Fresh-cut annual stems may root if you put them in a vase of clean water. But stems can root more reliably in a sterile, peat-based mix.

Have flowers blooming in sunny windows during fall and winter by starting new seedlings outdoors in pots in mid- to late summer. Bring them indoors several weeks before the first autumn frost.

SAVING SEEDS

Annuals make seeds, if allowed to, and they will grow for you. Watch the pods as they develop. They will often turn from green to tan as the seeds become ripe. Seeds are not viable unless they are fully formed. If the seedpods tend to open or even explode when ripe, slip a net of cheesecloth or a bit of old panty hose over them to trap the seeds. Store them in labeled envelopes for planting the next year. Seeds of biennials and, sometimes, hardy annuals, can be planted immediately.

They will begin to bloom as frost arrives, perfect for brightening the autumn transition period. This works well with French marigolds, pansies, petunias, nasturtiums, violas, impatiens, compact cockscomb, and annual asters. Simply discard the plants later when they get ratty looking.

SELF-SOWN ANNUALS

In informal gardens, plant non-hybrid annuals that may return from self-sown seeds allowed to mature and fall to the ground. Suitable annuals include the heirlooms love-lies-bleeding, love-in-a-mist, kiss-me-over-the-garden-gate, and cornflowers; wildflowers such as California poppies and verbenas; and open-pollinated annuals such as snapdragons, portulaca, cockscomb, and spider flowers.

Perennials

Perennials are distinct from annuals in that they return year after year, eliminating the need to buy and plant new flowers every spring. Unlike annuals, which often bloom all summer long, perennials generally bloom only one or, at the most, two seasons per year. There are spring bloomers, summer bloomers, and fall bloomers. When they're not in flower, perennials are enjoyed for their foliage, which is at least as important as the blooms.

DESIGNING WITH PERENNIALS

BLOOM SEQUENCE

The main difference between designing with annuals and designing with perennials is bloom sequence. Annuals tend to bloom all at once, but perennial plants bloom for only a short part of the growing season. One perennial follows another in the seasonal sequence of bloom, so the focus shifts as the garden changes. It is important to know when to expect each type of plant to flower and which ones will bloom at the same time.

■ Plan on a succession of bloom provided by different species if you would like flower color throughout the entire growing season. You can do this entirely with perennials, or mix in annuals for additional color midsummer to frost. Both tender (such as dahlia) and hardy (such as daffodil) bulbous plants offer additional possibilities. Throughout summer, hardy lilies—with their varied colors, heights, and forms—are especially effective in perennial borders.

■ Plan ahead to cover the gaps left by perennials that go dormant in summer. Two of the most common now-you-see-them-now-you-don't perennials are sun-loving Oriental poppies and shade-loving old-fashioned bleeding hearts. When done blooming, both plants slough off their old foliage and rest underground. This creates vacant places in the garden. But with a little planning, you can easily work around them.

• Plant Oriental poppies or bleeding hearts individually instead of in large clumps or drifts, which leave larger holes.

• Organize gardens so that neighboring plants can fill in and cover for the missing greenery. In shade, the ample foliage of hostas and

Old-fashioned bleeding hearts

Ferns add graceful foliage to gaps left by dormant perennials.

ferns can move into voids left when old-fashioned bleeding hearts go dormant. In sun, hardy geraniums, frothy baby's breath, and spreaders like dragon's blood sedum can fill in for Oriental poppies.

• Set a potted plant, such as a houseplant spending the summer outdoors, in the opening temporarily.

■ Observe your plantings through the seasons and note where color needs improved balance. Plant large blocks (at least three or more plants) of just a few varieties together, per bloom period. The bigger your garden, the larger these blocks of plants should be.

■ Note how the garden changes in both color scheme and balance from week to week. A yellow, blue, pale green, and white spring garden may transform into a red, purple, violet, and forest green one by July, and then go to gold, rusty red, purple, and bronze shades in September.

FORM

Plant shape is an important consideration when designing with perennials. If you select plants with varying forms, the garden will be more interesting. Ground-hugging mats; tall, spiked growth; and arching or rounded plants provide visual variety whether the plants are in bloom or not.

■ Many perennials fall into the following shape categories. But you should expect variations as the seasons progress. Perennials usually stretch up to flower and then fade back to their foliage after the bloom is through.

- Mats: Perennials such as lamium, bugleweed, and plumbago form low carpets suitable for ground covers or the front of the border.

- Mounds: Nicely rounded perennials such as coreopsis and hosta provide a soft look.

- Flower sprays with low foliage: Perennials such as yarrow, sea thrift, and coral bell bear taller flowers over neat low foliage. Height is dramatically reduced when

PERENNIALS WITH WIDE-RANGING FLOWER COLORS

Daylilies: pink, yellow, red, purple, cream

Iris: purple, red, yellow, white, blue

Lupines: yellow, red, pink, orange, blue

Lilies: pink, red, white, yellow

Poppies: pink, red, white, cream, orange

Phlox: pink, orange, purple, white, blue

Potentilla: pink, white, red, yellow

Peonies: white, pink, red, yellow

the old flower stems are removed.

• Vase shapes: When in bloom, plants such as garden phlox and Shasta daisies grow in an inverted triangular shape.

• Spikes: Plants such as salvia, lupine, gayfeather, and delphinium have slim, vertical flowering stems that contrast well with more horizontal forms.

■ Arrange the perennial garden so you can see and enjoy every plant—regardless of how small

Plant according to height so that all the flowers are visible.

it is. Place the tallest plants in the rear of a border that is viewed exclusively from the front. In an island bed viewed from all sides, place tall plants in the middle.

Work medium-height plants into the middle of a border or island bed, filling out the garden in front of the taller plants. Set small plants up front where they won't be hidden by taller leaves or flowers.

The neat progression of short to tall gives a garden a sense of order and tidiness many people appreciate. Don't be too rigid, however. You can work some medium-size varieties into the plants up front to add interest.

■ Bring a few tall plants forward to break up any tendency to make the garden profile too rigid. A garden can look more natural and interesting if it's allowed a few height variations. Here are some ideas to try:

• Plant some medium-height early bloomers such as columbines toward the front of the garden. They will flower before the other perennials are stirring and can be cut back after flowering so that only compact leaves remain.

• Swing an arc of medium-height plants up toward the front of the border, making a gentle curve that softens rigid organization

PERENNIALS THAT OFTEN NEED SUPPORT

Aster

Balloon flower

Bellflowers (tall types)

Foxglove

Garden phlox

Yarrow

Shasta daisy

Sedum (tall types)

Pyrethrum daisy

Hollyhock

Foxglove flowers often need support.

as boltonia and asters, yarrows and butterfly weed, or daisies and irises can result in pretty blends of flowers and foliage.

but doesn't extend so far into the front of the border that it becomes restrictive.

• Loop a small drift of shorter edging plants back into the medium-height flower section to ease the dividing line between the two.

■ Plant tall perennials together so they can support each other and thus need no staking. Combinations such

■ Lessen the impact of wind by planting tall perennials and ornamental grasses to shelter a garden full of more delicate plants. Sturdy-stemmed perennials, which are not likely to topple over with the first big gust, grow large enough to curb the wind faster than most shrubs and trees. Some perennials to try are maiden grasses, doe-pye weed, boltonia, goat's beard, and large hostas.

This tip also works on a smaller scale. You can plant smaller, delicate flowers beside sturdy medium-size plants like purple coneflowers and irises for wind protection.

TEXTURE

A variety of textures adds to a garden's beauty. Placing plants with feathery foliage next to ones with large, bold leaves will produce a more dramatic garden display.

■ To test how plants will look when planted together, place potted samples side by side and evaluate them.

■ Use plants with airy sprays of small flowers at the front of the garden. Perennials like baby's breath and coral bells have see-through veils of blossoms that don't obscure what's behind them. This can make the garden sparkle.

PATTERN

Some plants have foliage or flowers with stripes, spots, and splotches of color, which provide variety to the basic forms.

Fine textures are elegant in summer shade.

The drooping falls of dutch iris bear golden blazes.

Some flowers are two-toned, with outer petals of one color and inner ones of another, or with several colors on the same petal. Others, like iris, may have upper petals (standards) of one color and lower ones (falls) of another. Anthers or other flower parts may have colors that contrast with petals.

CARE AND FEEDING

PLANTING PERENNIALS

Unlike beds for annuals or vegetables, perennial beds are not dug up and replanted every year. Once perennials are planted, there will be no need to do more than routine weeding, feeding, cultivating, and mulching for several years. Learn how and when to do a few of the following maintenance tasks to ensure success with your perennials. This will almost certainly result in less work in the long run.

■ Choose healthy plants. For the inexperienced buyer, this may be easier said than done. In the spring, potted perennials may be showing only a little foliage, not providing much information about the health of the plant. Here are a few things you can do to get a better picture:

• Look at the plant's crown, the place where the shoots emerge from the soil. The emerging stems and leaves should be deep green, with no sign of wilting or rotting.

• Study the foliage and soil surface for signs of pests, which might be feeding on the crown, beneath the leaves, or fluttering up when you move the pot. If you find extensive evidence of pests, buy your plants elsewhere.

• Ask a salesclerk if you can look at the plant's roots. Turn the pot over and slip

Columbines live for only a couple of years, so allow a few plants to self-sow for continued stock.

the root-ball out. The roots should fill the pot, but not be crammed into it, and they should be healthy and firm.

■ Keep your expectations for plant life realistic. Although perennials like daylilies and hostas can live for decades, some perennials live only a few years. Perennials with short-but-sweet lives include columbine, blanketflower, and some chrysanthemums. Propagate new plants using division, cuttings, or seed to have replacements ready when needed.

■ Avoid wildflowers collected in the wild. Some people snatch wildflowers from native areas instead of propagating them in a nursery. This depletes the natural environment and can result in inferior plants not prepared for garden life. Be sure to buy wildflowers from a reputable garden center or nursery. Ask where they got the wildflowers and whether they were nursery propagated.

Be suspicious if you see pots with several small plants packed irregularly. They may have been taken from the wild. Flowers that are poorly rooted may have been recently dug and stuck in a pot. If you see wildflowers sold for less than a comparable perennial, it's a sign that they may have been harvested in the wild.

rows of petals, which form a full, fluffy-looking flower.

The big advantage of single-flowered peonies is weight. With fewer petals, the flowers stay lighter and are less likely to fall over when in full bloom. This means they don't need staking. The flowers are also less likely to trap moisture and, consequently, tend to suffer from fewer diseases.

■ Choose single-flowered peonies over the double-flowered types.

A single-flowered plant has a solitary row of petals (or several rows, in the case of peonies) around the perimeter of each blossom. Double-flowered plants have many

■ Choose disease-resistant cultivars of garden phlox and bee balm. Both perennials can be troubled with mildew diseases, which cover the plants with ugly white fuzz. Fortunately, developing disease-resistant cultivars has become a priority in the nursery industry. Check perennial catalogs to identify the best new cultivars for your climate.

■ Soak bare-root perennials in a bucket of water for an hour before planting. Bare roots have been out of their element (moist soil) while handled and shipped. Letting them soak up a little extra moisture can refresh moisture levels so the roots can grow vigorously in the weeks ahead.

■ Shape the planting hole to provide the proper support

Plant a disease-resistant cultivar of phlox.

for a bare-root perennial. When planting potted perennials, the shape of the pot is a good match for the hole you dig. But bare-root perennials tend to have octopuslike roots that need different treatment:

- Dig a wide, shallow hole in well-prepared soil.

- Form a cone of soil in the center of the hole. Make the cone high enough to hold the crown (where the shoots emerge from the roots) at the soil surface.

- Spread the roots around the perimeter of the cone so that each has its own space. Make sure the hole is deep enough to accommodate the entire root length without a lot of cramming, twisting, and turning.

- Fill in around the roots with soil, water well, and keep the soil moist.

■ Shake the potting mix off the roots of potted perennials and plant them like bare-root perennials. Larger perennials sold in 1- or 2-quart-size containers are perfect candidates for this. The reason for doing this is that peat potting mixes can complicate plant establishment in the soil. The roots of perennials grown in peat-based mixes can have difficulty growing out of the peat and into the native soil. In addition, peat can quickly become parched in drying soils, causing root

Purple coneflowers tolerate drought.

DROUGHT-TOLERANT PERENNIALS

■ Yarrow

■ Artemisia

■ Butterfly weed

■ Sea pink

■ Orange coneflower

■ Purple coneflower

■ Gayfeather

■ Lavender

■ Russian sage

■ Sedum

■ Yucca

Elongated leaf tips help to shed excess water.

■ Use plants adapted to dry conditions in drought-prone climates. Perennials such as butterfly weed have deep or moisture-storing roots that allow them to weather dry conditions. Other drought-tolerant plants have leaves that are modified to reduce moisture loss. Silver leaves reflect hot sunlight, and needle-shape leaves have less surface area for moisture loss. Moisture is stored inside succulent leaves, and moisture loss from furry leaves is slowed by their coating.

damage. Getting the peat out eliminates both of these problems and can help new perennials get established faster than you ever thought possible.

Goat's beard can be difficult to move, so plant it properly from the start.

■ Space large, slow-growing perennials properly at the start. Big hostas, goat's beard, and gas plants, for example, can be hard to move once they are established. Ask at the nursery, consult the plant label, or check a garden encyclopedia for information on how big the plant will get.

Then be sure to allow enough space for the plant to reach its mature limits without overcrowding.

■ Use salt-tolerant perennials in cold-climate roadside plantings. Roads heavily salted during winter snowstorms often leave salt residue in the soil. Perennials such as sea thrifts, bearberry, and rugosa roses thrive in soils that are salty enough to kill other plants.

KEEPING THINGS TIDY

■ Support full, floppy perennials with pruned twigs. This is an old British trick called *pea staking*. It helps perennials stay upright and look natural without glaring metallic stakes or forced shapes that result from corseting with twine. Even better, pea staking costs nothing but a little time.

When the perennials begin to arise in spring, set the ends of sturdy branched twigs around the plant. The twigs should be about as long as the height of the perennial. As the stems grow, they will fill out to hide the twigs. You can cut off any errant woody stems that remain in sight after the perennial reaches full height.

■ Pinch asters and mums to make them more compact and bushy. Pinching is one of the handiest things you can do in the garden. Removing the stem tip, with a pinch of your fingernails or with pruning shears.

Pinching is particularly helpful for mums and asters. Flowering plants purchased in a pot have been specially treated to make the plants bushy and full. If left untouched the following year, they will grow fewer, taller, scraggly stems that are more likely to need staking for support.

When pinching, scheduling is important. You want to start early enough to make an

impact. And you need to stop by July 1 so flower buds can develop before cold strikes. Use the following pinching schedule to get started with mums, but feel free to modify it as you gain experience:

- Pinch shoot tips when the stems are 4 to 6 inches high.

- Pinch again three weeks later.

- Pinch a final time in late June if necessary.

■ Shear reblooming perennials such as catmint and 'moonbeam' coreopsis to promote a second flush of flowers. Getting rid of the old

Cut the old flowers off reblooming perennials to encourage new growth.

flowers and seedpods encourages new growth, new buds, and new flowers. This is a great reward for a small amount of effort.

■ Use a string trimmer to cut back ornamental grasses in spring. The golden leaves and seed plumes are a great winter attraction. But in spring, the old growth must be removed before the new shoots begin to sprout. The string trimmer quickly cuts through thin grass stems. Rake them up and toss them on the compost pile—job finished!

■ Renew a declining clump of perennials by division. As many perennials grow, new shoots emerge at the perimeter of the clump, which keeps spreading outward. The center becomes increasingly older— sometimes woody, sometimes completely barren.

The solution is division. In spring, late summer, or fall, dig up the entire clump. Cut out the old heart, refresh the soil with organic matter, and replant healthy young pieces. You may have enough good divisions left to share with friends.

LOW-MAINTENANCE TECHNIQUES

■ Convert your front yard into a cottage garden. Tending flowers is much more fun than mowing grass!

A well-tended cottage garden serves as an attractive front yard.

■ Make an artificial bog for plants that need constantly wet soil. Then you will be able to grow water-loving plants such as swamp irises, variegated cattails, and ligularias.

Begin by deciding where you want the bog garden to be located. They are natural companions for fountains, water gardens, bridges, or streams. Dig out a deep trench (2 to 3 feet deep) or swale for the bog garden, then line the hole with plastic. Set a perforated hose in the bottom, with an end emerging from one side to connect with your household hose. Fill the hole with rich soil, and plant bog natives. You can irrigate through the submerged hose as needed to keep the garden constantly moist.

■ Plant perennials instead of grass in the boulevard strip. The boulevard strip is the public space located between the sidewalk and the road. It can be hot, dry, and heavily trod upon. This makes it difficult to keep grass looking healthy and nice.

Instead of fighting a constant battle with turf, use a different tactic. Plant the boulevard strip with low but bushy perennials that people won't walk on. Choose heat- and drought-tolerant perennials such as coreopsis, 'Silver Mound' artemisia, and sea thrift. Now the problem area can become a pretty garden.

PERENNIALS IN THE SHADE

■ Start a shade garden under trees by adding 4 inches of compost over the tree roots before planting. Rich, moist

PERENNIALS FOR BOGGY SOIL

Calla lily	Japanese iris
Canna	Ligularia
Cardinal flower	Louisiana iris
Primroses	Rodgersia

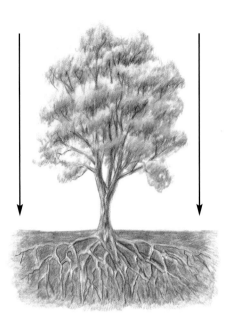

compost provides a fast start for newly planted perennials. This is important—the flowers need to be growing strongly before tree roots move in and capitalize on their growing space. Compost also helps keep the garden moist in summer, when the trees and perennials may compete for water. Be careful when planting not to damage the tree roots, but be sure to get the new roots into the soil below the compost.

PERENNIALS FOR DEEP SHADE

Ajuga

Bleeding heart

Brunnera

Dead nettle

Epimedium

Ferns (evergreen types)

Hosta

Jack-in-the-pulpit

Virgina bluebell

Wild ginger

Wild violet

■ Avoid dense tree roots by planting a shade garden around the outside of the tree canopy rather than directly underneath. Many tree roots cluster under the branch canopy, and active feeding goes on near the drip line— the place where rainwater drips off the leafy branch tips. Gardening beyond the shadow of the limbs reduces root competition, and the plants will get more light.

■ Plant shade-loving perennials on the shady north side of shrubs if you don't have trees. Perennials such as anemones, astilbes, hostas, Lenten roses, and violets can look lovely against a backdrop of evergreen shrubs. Flowering deciduous shrubs such as viburnums or hydrangeas can be even more beautiful.

Buying bulbs in bulk may save you money.

BULBS IN THE PERENNIAL GARDEN

WHAT IS A BULB?

In everyday language, any plant with an underground storage organ is referred to as a *bulb*, even at garden centers. There are many categories, technically speaking, with different names for different structures.

TRUE BULBS

True bulbs, such as tulips, are made of modified leaves that are attached to a flat basal plate. They surround the following season's flower bud. Some bulbs (such as daffodils and tulips) are surrounded by a papery tunic, and some (such as lilies) are covered by fleshy scales.

CORMS

Corms look much like bulbs but when cut open, they have a solid starchy interior stem. Crocuses grow from corms.

TUBERS

Tubers are modified stems with starchy interiors but no basal plate or tunic. Both roots and shoots sprout from the same growth buds, called *eyes*. The potato is a typical tuber. *Tuberous roots* are similar but are actually swollen roots, not stems. Dahlias produce tuberous roots. *Rhizomes* are thickened underground stems. They grow in a horizontal manner, sprouting new sections as they spread. The bearded iris is a typical rhizome.

GARDENING WITH BULBS

■ Plant spring-flowering bulbs to give early seasonal color to lifeless perennial beds. While the perennials are just beginning to stir and arise, the spring-flowering bulbs are decked with color. As the bulbs are fading, the perennials are beginning to come on strong. It is an ideal partnership.

Daffodils (back) bloom a little earlier than tulips (center) and hyacinths (front).

As these tulips fade, the irises are ready to bloom in their place.

■ Plan ahead to find the best place for interplanting bulbs with perennials. Although they bloom in the spring, early flowering bulbs must be planted in the fall. They look best set in clumps around or between perennials such as hardy geraniums, daylilies, and Siberian irises that don't need frequent division (which would disrupt the bulbs).

Don't wait until the bulbs arrive in October. Mark ideal planting places with a tag or stake in spring or summer, when your existing bulbs are blooming and clumps of perennials are still small. Later in the autumn, when the perennials are dormant, you'll already have the best planting places marked.

PURCHASING BULBS

■ Choose healthy bulbs. Use the same criteria you would use if shopping for good-quality onions in the grocery store.

- Look for plump bulbs without soft spots or dark diseased blotches.

- Check the basal plate, where the roots will emerge. It should be firm and undamaged.

- Daffodil bulbs with two noses will provide twice the bloom, but tulip bulbs should have only one nose. With two, they won't flower.

■ Combine bulb orders with your friends to buy wholesale and save money. One catalog offers 100 tulip bulbs for just a few dollars more than 50 tulip bulbs. You should order early to ensure the best selection and prompt delivery.

PLANTING BULBS

■ Soak fall-planted bulbs in warm water for 12 hours before planting. This moisturizing method works with tunicate-type bulbs (neatly enclosed round or teardrop-shape bulbs) and is not suitable for lily or other bulbs with loose, fleshy scales. Soaking allows suitable bulbs to absorb enough water to begin growth immediately, saving two or three weeks of time. This is particularly helpful in northern climates, where early arriving winter weather limits leisurely rooting.

■ Add liquid rodent repellent to bulb-soaking water (at the lowest recommended concentration) to make the treated bulbs unappetizing to rodents.

Bitter-tasting rodent repellent is absorbed by the bulbs, which then become unattractive to mice,

chipmunks, rabbits, raccoons, skunks, and most other animals. It's particularly helpful for crocuses and other edible, shallowly planted bulbs that are easily unearthed and eaten by passing critters.

■ Plant a double layer of 'Paper White' narcissus bulbs for twice the flower display. 'Paper White' narcissus, with sweetly scented clusters of small white daffodil flowers, are warm-climate bulbs that naturally bloom during winter. Pot them in late fall or

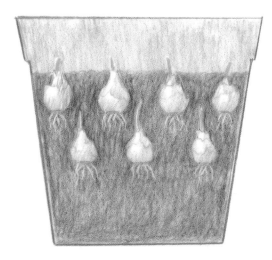

early winter, and then watch them come to life in a sunny window, even as the snow falls outside.

■ Most people plant five or six bulbs in an 8-inch bulb pot or forcing dish, which makes a nice enough display. But if you can find a deeper nursery pot, you can plant a bottom and top layer of bulbs to produce awe-inspiring results. Here's how:

- Put several inches of moist peat-based potting mix in the bottom of a deep pot.

- Set bulbs in the mix, with the flat rooting plate down and the pointed nose up. Put the bulbs side by side around the perimeter of the pot and fill the center with one or several bulbs (the actual number will vary depending on the size of the pot).

- Cover the lower-level bulbs with an inch or two of moist potting mix.

- Set the upper layer of bulbs in this mix, positioning them between (not over) the sprouting noses of the lower-level bulbs.

- Cover the upper level with potting mix, allowing any lanky green sprouts to emerge uncovered.

- Set the potted bulbs in a cool location to root for several weeks. Keep the soil moist but not wet. Then bring the pot into a warm, sunny window and let the growth begin!

■ Plant a triple layer of bulbs in the garden. The technique is similar to that above but the characters differ.

Plant a shallow layer of early bloomers like crocuses, snowdrops, or squills for early spring color. Just below them, planted about 5 or 6 inches deep, put daffodils that bloom in mid-spring. Underneath the daffodils, plant late-blooming tulips, which benefit from deep planting and finish up the flower display. You can also plant up a large pot for a burst of early color.

■ Make intensive bulb plantings work

smoothly by discouraging competition and disease spread. Use only well-drained soil for bulbs. In wet soils, bulbs will rot. Plan to fertilize in the fall with a product formulated for bulbs so they won't have to compete for

In a small garden, bulbs in pots make an ongoing spring statement.

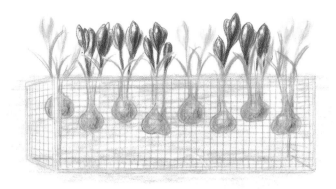

nutrients. Water during spring while bulbs are actively growing, but allow the soil to dry out in summer when they are dormant.

■ Discourage rodents from eating crocuses and other bulbs by planting them in fine-mesh wire baskets. If animals can't dig the bulbs out, they can't eat them. Wire cages also help prevent accidental human damage with shovels and hoes.

BULBS NOT PRONE TO RODENT ATTACKS

■ Squills
■ Flowering onions
■ Colchicums (autumn bloomers)
■ Crown imperial
■ Daffodils (narcissus); also called jonquils

■ Plant tulips 8 to 10 inches deep to prolong their life and protect them from rodents. When set deep, tulip bulbs are slower to split and stop flowering. It also takes some serious digging for rodents to reach them. It's a win-win situation.

■ Plant the same cultivar of daffodil together in groups of 10, 20, or more. Then all the flowers will bloom together— at the same time, in the same

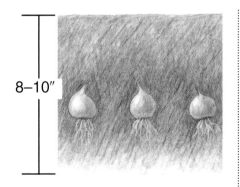

8–10″

color—making a maximum impact. Just a few daffodils look lonely, and a clump of mixed colors and cultivars looks chaotic.

■ Divide or fertilize crowded daffodils to increase their

bloom. Daffodils that have multiplied to form a large clump may have depleted the soil nutrients and riddled all the rooting space in the process. The result may be plenty of green leaves but few or no flowers. The solution is as easy as fertilizer or as down-to-earth as division. Start by applying fertilizer. Slow-release bulb fertilizers can be used in fall for good root growth and continued

Daffodils make a big splash when planted in larger groups.

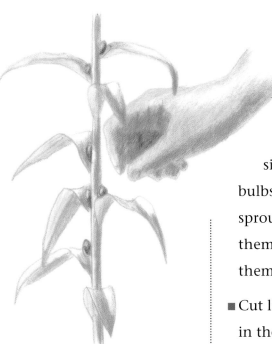

them to make new plants. These bulbils look like small, dark berries but contain no seeds at all. They are similar to miniature bulbs and have the ability to sprout into new plants. Give them a chance, and watch them grow.

■ Cut lily stems to the ground in the fall to avoid stem rot.

■ Mark the location of bulbs with a stake, stick, rock, or tag so you know where they are while they're dormant. Without an above-ground reminder, it's easy to dig into the bulbs by mistake when planting other flowers or vigorously hoeing out weeds.

■ Cover large patches of bulbs with a ground cover that will fill the void when the

effectiveness in early spring. Or you can use an all-purpose, balanced fertilizer when growth begins in the spring.

To divide daffodils, dig up the bulbs as the foliage fades. Separate tightly packed clusters, refresh the soil with organic matter, and replant with generous spacing.

■ Remove the bulbils, or secondary bulbs, from the stems of lilies and plant bulbs go dormant. Bulbs brighten the ground cover in spring, and the ground cover helps keep the bulbs cool and dry in summer. You may need to fertilize more often since twice the plants will be growing in the same space.

■ Customize bulbs and ground covers by considering their height, sturdiness, and foliage thickness.

Bicolored species tulips and snow-in-summer

Bulbs with weak stems cannot emerge through heavy-leafed ground covers such as pachysandra. Small-leafed ground covers with more open growth, such as periwinkle, can be more suitable.

SOME TULIPS WITH HANDSOME, COLORED FOLIAGE

Greigii tulips

'Donna Bella'

'Red Riding Hood'

'Grand Prestige'

'Margaret Herbst'

'Oratorio'

Species tulips

Tulipa linifolia

Tulipa maximowiczii

Fosteriana tulips

'Easter Moon'

'Juan'

Kaufmanniana tulips

'Showwinner'

'Johann Strauss'

Bulbs must be tall enough to grow up and over any ground cover surrounding them. Short, early spring bloomers like crocuses may be better placed with deciduous ground covers like epimedium (which die back to the ground in winter) than with ever-green ground covers such as pachysandra.

■ Leave bulb foliage loose to ripen properly. Cutting off the foliage before it yellows severs the bulbs' food supply and weakens them. Putting daffodils in bondage by tying up their leaves also reduces food production and can make them more prone to disease attack. Taking care of bulb foliage, even though the bloom is gone, helps ensure more flowers in the years to come.

■ Cut the tall, spent stems of tulip flowers down to the first leaf. This removes the old flower and also leaves the

attractive broad foliage to ripen in the garden as nature intended.

∎ Brighten dull spots in the garden with pots of tender bulbs such as agapanthus, tuberous begonias, caladiums, pineapple lilies, or tuberoses. The versatility of pots combined with the bright blooms of summer-flowering bulbs keeps gardens looking exceptional all summer and fall.

∎ Store tender bulbs in vermiculite or peat to keep them from drying out. These materials are a packing cushion and more. They help keep the bulbs from drying out and rotting. Peat moss, which naturally suppresses disease, is particularly good for this job.

• Dig the bulbs when the soil is relatively dry so they won't emerge caked with mud.

• Gently brush off any extra soil, and remove any old vegetation. Throw out any damaged bulbs.

• Prepare a place for winter storage. Place a layer of vermiculite or peat in the bottom of a plastic storage box. Store one kind of bulb per box or one kind per layer, making sure to label each layer so you know which is which next spring.

• Set the bulbs in the peat or vermiculite, keeping them an inch or two away from each other.

• Cover with a thick layer of peat or vermiculite and add another group of bulbs, repeating this process until all are packed.

• Store in a cool (but not cold) place during winter.

• Check the bulbs at least once a month (preferably more often). Remove any that may have rotted. If all the bulbs begin to shrivel, dampen the packing medium slightly to prevent further moisture loss.

■ Divide dahlias to make more plants every year. Dahlias contain underground food-storing tuberous roots, which look a little like a potato. The swollen roots connect to a central stalklike crown, which contains all the growth buds.

Look closely to find the small scaly bumps or sprouts that indicate where a new shoot will arise. Both roots and shoots are necessary for a new division to succeed.

In the spring, take dahlia roots out of storage. Cut the crown longitudinally into several pieces, each with at least one root and growth bud. Now each division can act as an independent plant.

■ Prestart dahlias indoors six weeks before the last spring

frost arrives so you can have extra-early flowers.

- Plant the tuberous roots in large nursery pots filled with compost-enriched, peat-based potting mix.

- Put the pots in a warm, bright location. The plants will root and sprout.

- Dahlias can stay in large pots all summer, as long as you keep the soil moist and add extra fertilizer. Or you can transplant them outdoors into the garden when the danger of spring frosts pass.

■ Dig cold-sensitive tropical bulbs such as cannas and caladiums before the first fall frost to prevent damage to the bulbs. Damaged bulbs are likely to rot in winter storage.

■ Dig cold-tolerant tender bulbs such as dahlias and gladiolus

In pots or in the ground, dahlias are dramatic in summer.

Long-stemmed tulips are wonderful flowers to cut and bring indoors.

after a light frost has killed the foliage.

■ Point the shovel blade—not the handle—straight down into the soil when digging bulbs. This prevents the shovel from angling into nearby bulbs and slicing them in half.

Ground Covers, Vines, and Roses

Herbs and vegetables, annual and perennial flowers—these garden mainstays are often a central focus of any landscape plan. However, if you really want to make the very most of your garden, you might also want to consider such plantings as ground covers, vines, and roses. Just because these elements may seem fancy doesn't mean you can't grow them beautifully—and easily.

GROUND COVERS

DESIGN DETAILS

Ground covers are perennial plants or, sometimes, low-growing shrubs that form a stable, solid mat of growth, replacing either lawn or garden beds. The lawn itself is one kind of ground cover that is a landscaping standby, even in areas where it is not that easy to keep lawn grass alive. It is best not to mix too many kinds of ground covers into the same area, for they will spread and become intermixed in a way that is hard to handle.

No one can give you a list of all possible ground-cover plants. Ground covering is a way of using plants, not the plants themselves. To function well, a ground cover should grow thickly enough to block out most competing weeds,

Ground covers can be used in masses or lines. This edging of liriope makes a trim and attractive finish between the brick walk and the lawn.

look good for all or most of the year, prevent erosion, and not be in constant need of repositioning. There are flowering and nonflowering ground covers. Many ground covers are tough enough to grow in root-filled soil in shade under trees.

■ Ground covers can be taller or shorter, as you please. Typically, ground covers should not be used in dinky clumps. Rather, mass them generously over wider areas for visual appearance and easy maintenance.

■ Plant ground cover in a spot that is difficult to mow or hard to use for grass or other plants because of tree roots or shade.

■ Plant ground cover in pockets of soil between tree roots (see illustration on page 250). Soil pockets are easiest to find near the trunk of the tree, where roots have become stout and no longer riddle the earth. Just add some organic matter, as necessary, to get ground cover off to a good start, and then water as needed during dry weather.

Pocket plantings are great places to try less common and especially beautiful ground covers like European or American gingers, epimedium, and golden star.

PLANTING GROUND COVER

Ground-cover plantings should be evenly thick. It helps to set plants in place at regular spacing in the first place. Begin by preparing the ground as for any garden bed. Then use a wire or string grid with regularly spaced openings at three-inch intervals (or other size if appropriate) to

Ground covers are often used to fill spots that are difficult to mow or are barren of grass and other plants because of tree roots or shade.

help you distribute the plants. For easier, trouble-free planting, consider the following tips:

■ Use landscape fabric instead of plastic to reduce weeds in large plantings. Landscape fabric has pores that allow free air and water movement a big advantage over impen-etrable plastic. Lay it down before planting and then cut holes in the fabric. Plant your ground cover in the holes. When covered with mulch, landscape fabric prevents light from reaching the soil, which will stop the sprouting of most weed seeds.

A GIFT OF GROUND COVER

Ground covers spread fast. People with established gardens often have ground cover to spare, because it needs thinning or trimming. See if a neighboring gardener or even a groundskeeper at the park will fill a big plastic trash bag with starts of wild ginger, epimedium, or pachysandra for you. It will save you some serious money, compared to buying flats at the garden center or hiring a landscaper to do the job.

openings and allow it to spread until it fills out the slope.

■ Set ground cover plugs in place using a wire grid stretched over the bed for fast, easy planting. The regularly spaced openings will help you to coordinate spacing without a measuring tape.

■ Help ground covers spread by layering stems as they grow. Layering encourages stems to root while still connected to the parent plant.

Ground covers such as pachysandra are easily rooted simply by covering barren portions of the stem with soil and keeping them moist. For harder-to-root ground covers such as wintercreeper, you can remove a small piece of bark from the bottom of the stem and treat the opening with rooting hormone before covering the stem with soil.

■ Hold barren soil in place with burlap when planting ground cover on a slope. This will prevent erosion while the ground cover is getting established. You should pin the burlap securely into the soil so that it won't slip off when rain makes the soil heavy and wet. Cut modest openings in the burlap and plant one ground cover in each.

Once the ground cover establishes a strong root system and is able to secure nearby soil from erosion, you can gradually enlarge the

■ Spread netting or old sheets over ground covers during autumn leaf drop. It can be difficult to rake leaves out of thick ground covers, and allowing the leaves to sit and mat on the ground-cover bed creates unhealthy conditions. But planning ahead to catch leaves as they fall allows you to gather up all the leaves in one easy move and keeps the ground cover uncluttered.

■ Rejuvenate winter-burned ground-cover plantings by mowing. If a cold winter causes broad-leaf evergreens to grow brown and unsightly,

GROUND COVER FOR SHADY PLACES

Boston ivy

Virginia creeper

Wintercreeper

Lily of the valley

Dead nettle

Sedges

Wild ginger

Golden star

Epimedium

Sweet woodruff

Pachysandra

Woodland phlox

Hardy geraniums (some
  species)

Ground covers can replace turf grass in some situations, but it takes proper care to keep them tidy.

don't give up hope. There is a good chance that the roots are still alive and will send up fresh green growth come springtime. Mowing off the old leaves gives the new leaves plenty of space and keeps the bed tidy.

VINES

GETTING STARTED WITH CLIMBING PLANTS

Climbing plants are ideal for landscaping because you can effectively plan for and limit their size. Their eventual heights and widths are determined by the structures on which they are grown. The structures themselves fill the space before the vines or climbers have reached full growth. Be careful not to let vines escape their bounds by climbing into nearby trees. Clinging vines can damage the house structure by working their roots into the mortar, if it is weak. It's better to train vines up trellises set about a foot away from the house.

Honeysuckle makes both a good ground cover and climbing vine.

There are many different kinds of vines, and they climb in different ways:

■ Twining vines need something to twist around. The new growth twists onto supports as it grows. Sturdy poles and pergolas make good supports. Examples are kiwi, bougainvillea, American bittersweet, morning glory, honeysuckle, American wisteria, and black-eyed Susan vine. All of these can grow prodigiously in a single season.

■ Vines with tendrils need slender strings, wires, or narrow supports to grasp onto. Examples are clematis, passionflower, and grape. They are easy to train, but do not let them start climbing into trees. They can be used to beautify chain-link fences but need additional wires or trellising to grow on wooden fences.

■ Clinging vines stick to solid objects. These vines work their aerial roots into the smallest of crevices in solid walls. They can damage some kinds of walls, especially brick walls with old mortar that is beginning to weaken, but are safe to grow if the wall is sound. Do not grow them on surfaces that need to be painted from time to time. Clinging vines are fine on other walls and sturdy supports. These vines include climbing hydrangea, trumpet creeper, and winter-creeper.

BEAUTY WITH PURPOSE

Vines do double-duty in a garden. Flowers, foliage, or fruit make them spectacular vertical accents to train on a fence, trellis, or lamppost. As an added bonus, vines can hide unsightly eyesores, provide shade, and blend tree trunks, walls, and fences into the scenery with a patina of greenery.

Decorative vines, such as this purple clematis, can be trained to climb fences and trellises, creating living walls of bright color.

Use your imagination to create a dramatic garden centerpiece.

sometimes beyond. In contrast, many of the tallest perennials reach their maximum height only when in flower, which may last for just a few weeks. Here are some support options to consider:

- Wire cages: These work like tomato cages but can be made from wire mesh in any height or shape. A narrow, upright pillar shape is elegant in a formal garden.

- Tepees: Make a support of angled posts tied together at the top. Plant one or several vines at the base and let them twine up and fill out to cover the post.

- Scrims: These are open-structured, see-through supports that vines can climb and still provide a veiled view of the scene beyond. With imagination,

■ Add height to a perennial border with annual or perennial vines on wire cages, tepees, or scrims. When you want a dynamic high point for a flower garden, an upward-trained vine will be effective throughout the growing season and

Decorate an old tree stump with a colorful vine such as clematis.

4 feet apart, pounding their bases about 10 inches deep into the ground. Run the twine between the posts, knotting it around the posts occasionally to keep the twine from slipping down. You may want to make vertical webbing by working the twine up and down between horizontal strands, which helps some vines climb more efficiently.

Plant annual vines such as sweet peas, cardinal climbers, or black-eyed Susan beneath the new trellis, and allow them to grow and cover it. When frost arrives or the vines begin to look shabby, simply cut off the twine trellis and throw it, vines and all, in the compost pile.

scrims can be made of braided wire or other creative materials.

■ Try an extra-easy way to support annual vines with a trellis made from biodegradable twine. Set two 4-foot-high posts about

■ Create summer shade on a porch with a string trellis covered with vines. String trellises, available from garden centers or mail-order garden catalogs, can be hung from a roof or held upright with posts. Set the trellis to the south or west side of the porch to block the most sun.

■ Use a wire trellis and vines to cover a blank, dull wall or a utility pipe. A trellis-covered wall comes to life with greenery. Just make sure the trellis is far enough away from the wall; a trellis snug against a wall is not good for either the building or the vines. If you are

screening a utility pipe, be sure to leave access openings for maintenance.

■ Use vines to cover a chain-link fence or other backyard eyesore. Vines can screen off your garage (or your

Hide an unattractive utility pipe with a trellis of dazzling vines.

An ugly chain-link fence becomes a lush green wall when it's covered with vines.

blooms. Just as grapevines in the woods can cover trees and turn them into a dripping mass of green vines, an old stump can become a garden pillar.

In mild climates, evergreen vines can provide reliable cover year-round. In cold climates, some evergreen vines can be more prone to dieback when temperatures really

neighbor's garage) from view, make a hidden alcove for your garbage cans, or cover a bare tree trunk or a fenced dog run. Remember to plant vines that twine or have tendrils on open supports like chain-link fencing and vines that climb on solid supports like walls.

■ Use vines to make a dead tree disappear into a mass of

This open pergola frame is covered with Chinese wisteria.

drop. Look for extra-hardy vines for this job.

■ Plant vines on an open pergola frame to create a cool, shaded retreat. A pergola is an arborlike structure with an overhead trellis that forms a garden roof. It can make a shady place to sit outside in summer and give the garden elegant architecture at the same time.

To fill out the roof with foliage and flowers, try planting vines that have abundant growth so they will be well able to go the distance needed. Some possibilities are wisteria, silver fleece vine, kiwi, hops, and grapes.

ROSES

Roses have been improved from disease-ridden, one-shot wonders to floriferous denizens. The earliest roses usually bloomed only once a year, but they gave off wonderful aromas. Old-fashioned roses can grow into large, thorny bushes, more vigorous than a modern hybrid tea rose.

In the early 1800s, reblooming roses from China were discovered and interbred with old-fashioned European roses to extend their bloom period. These hybrids had fewer thorns and petals but rebloomed through the summer. Breeding efforts focused on improving flower form and expanding color selection. The results were grandifloras, hybrid teas, and other long-blooming plants that required high maintenance.

To create hardier roses that need less spraying, have more fragrance, and bloom all summer, breeders began to infuse bloodlines of the old-fashioned roses back into modern hybrids. This has created landscape roses, large or small bushes that

The rose, one of the most popular flowers, is celebrated in song and verse.

bloom all season and have increased disease resistance. Many, but not all, are fragrant.

■ Choose shrub roses over hybrid tea roses for low maintenance and disease resistance. Look for the following brands of high-quality shrub roses: David Austin English roses (from England), Town and Country Roses (from Denmark), Meidiland Romantica roses (from France), rugosa roses (developed from Oriental Rosa rugosa), and Explorer roses (extra-hardy hybrids from Ottawa Experiment Station in Canada).

David Austin English shrub roses are floriferous and fragrant.

■ Protect a rose graft, the swollen knob near the base of the plant, from winter damage. Not all roses have grafts, but most hybrid teas, grandifloras, standard (tree form), and some miniatures are grafted. When planting, check for the graft and make arrangements to keep it from harm, if necessary. Here are several options:

- In well-drained soil, you can plant the rose deeper than in heavy soil, covering the graft with insulating soil. In cold climates, the graft union should be planted 2 to 3 inches below the soil line.

- Mound soil up over the graft in late fall and pull it back in spring.

- Surround the graft with shredded leaves, and hold the leaves in place with wire mesh.

- Buy plastic foam rose cones to insulate the entire plant once it is dormant.

■ Take good care of your roses so they will stay relatively free

of pests and diseases. Roses can be susceptible to a wide variety of problems, especially if they are growing weakly. Make sure they have well-drained, fertile soil. Water roses during dry weather and mulch them to conserve moisture. Prune to ensure each cane receives sun and good air circulation. With this kind of treatment, problems will be few and far between.

■ Prune hybrid teas, floribundas, and other roses

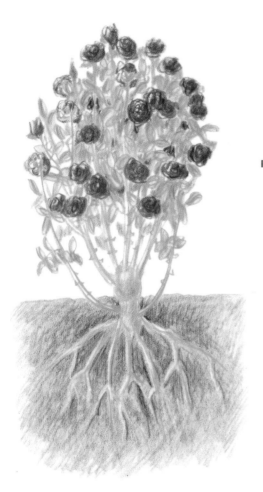

canes. For shrub roses, pruning can be as simple as cutting out old and dead canes with long-handled pruning loppers.

■ Remove root suckers from grafted roses to keep them true. Many hybrid tea and floribunda roses are grafted on the extra-vigorous and disease-resistant roots of other species such as multiflora or rugosa roses. These rootstocks may send up sprouts of their own, called *suckers,* which are easily identified by the different-looking foliage and flowers. Upon close inspection, you can see root suckers emerge from below the swollen graft. Clip suckers back as soon as you see them to keep the inferior sprouts from competing with your rose cultivar.

requiring heavy shaping back to 12 inches tall while they are dormant in spring. These roses flower on new growth, and nothing encourages new growth more than heavy spring pruning. While you are cutting stems back, take some time to remove any dead, diseased, or overcrowded

If the only sprouts that arise from the plant are off the roots, the graft has been

Preventive measures will keep black spot away from your roses.

damaged—which can occur during winter—and the original rose top is dead. If the root is a rugosa rose, you might try to grow it—it's a pretty plant. But if the root is a multiflora rose, it is a weed that is best taken out early.

■ Control black spot by planning ahead. Black spot, which marks leaves with black spots and then kills them, can spread up the plant and cause complete defoliation. Its damage is not pretty! But it can be avoided. Buy disease-resistant roses, including many of the landscape roses, polyantha roses such as 'The Fairy,' and even disease-resistant hybrid tea roses like 'Olympiad.' Sprays with baking soda can prevent black spot infection. Simply mix 2 teaspooons baking soda in 2 quarts water

Roses come in a wide range of vivid colors—as well as pastels.

fragrant herbs such as mint, sweet marjoram, oregano, thyme, bush basil, and German chamomile. These herbs provide an attractive cover for the barren bases of many roses

with ½ teaspoon corn oil. Shake well, put in a sprayer, and go to work. Even disease-resistant shrub roses can benefit from this in extra-humid or wet weather.

Rake up and destroy any leaves infested with black spot. This helps eliminate spores that would otherwise reinfect healthy leaves.

■ Plant around rose bushes with low or medium-height

and release an odor that can screen the plant from rose-eating pests. They will also provide a nice harvest for the kitchen. Forget about eating the herbs, however, if you spray the rose with chemicals unsuited for edible plants.

■ Layer ramblers and other roses to make new plants. Ramblers have long, limber canes that can be tied to a fence or trellis like a climbing rose. These flexible canes make them perfect for layering. Notch the bark beneath the stem, remove nearby leaves, pin the stem to the ground, and mound over it with soil.

Once rooted and cut free from the mother plant, you'll have a new plant growing on its own roots. It will have no need for graft protection!

■ Use the Minnesota tip method in cold climates for winter protection of hybrid tea roses. In well-drained soil, dig a trench on one side of the rose. With your foot, gently push the rose canes into the trench, where they will be insulated underground. Mound soil over the canes and graft and mark the burial site with a stake so you can free the canes in early spring.

CLASSIC OLD-FASHIONED ROSES

Alba roses

'Semi Plena'

'Konigin von Danemark'

Bourbon roses

'Louise Odier'

'Variegata de Bologna'

'Madame Isaac Pereire'

'Honorine de Brabant'

Centrifolia roses

'De Meaux'

Damask roses

'Madame Hardy'

'Comte de Chambord'

'Celsiana'

Gallica roses

Rosa gallica officinalis

'Cardinal de Richelieu'

Moss roses

'Mundi'

'Empress Josephine'

Shrubs and Flowering Trees

Shrubs and trees are relatively permanent landscape features that need little care. In return, they provide shade, privacy, and beauty with their flowers, berries, form, and foliage. Choose the right plantings for your site, and you'll find that everything falls together quite nicely.

SHRUBS

DESIGN DETAILS

While you may think of shrubs as "just green bushes," they are actually much more. Shrubs come in a variety of shapes and sizes, with many different types of foliage. Some shrubs produce berries, and others even provide fragrance! No matter what effect you are trying to achieve, there is undoubtedly a shrub that will fit the bill.

Creeping shrubs, like junipers, can serve as evergreen ground covers. Low, bushy

This shrub garden looks dazzling in any season.

From subtle shades of green to dazzling purples, yellows, and reds, a remarkable variety of woody plants is available to satisfy every need.

shrubs like spirea and potentilla blend nicely into flower gardens or the front of a planting around the house. Larger, rounded shrubs can be grouped into clusters to define space or create privacy. More compact cultivars that mature when around 4 feet high, like 'Newport' viburnum, can be used around a house without any pruning. Taller shrubs, like Allegheny viburnum, are best kept at some distance from the house where they won't block the views. They make good screens for the property perimeter. Vertical shrubs that are shaped like an upright cone or pillar, such as 'Skyrocket' juniper, create formality or emphasis in the yard. They can be striking when placed on either side of a doorway or garden gate.

Using a medley of shrub shapes creates design interest that goes much deeper than the leaves and flowers. And when you also take into account the other qualities shrubs have to offer, you'll see that they are an asset to any kind of garden.

■ Plant fragrant flowered shrubs near doors or windows so you can enjoy their perfume both indoors and out.

■ Cut flowering stems from your shrubs and bring them indoors to use in big bouquets. If you have large vases that dwarf ordinary annual or perennial stems, fill them with long

SOME SHRUBS WITH FRAGRANT FLOWERS

Butterfly bush

Blue spiraea

Summersweet

Fothergilla

Daphne

Fantasy lilac

Dwarf Korean lilac

Miss Kim lilac

French lilac

Witch hazel

Burkwood viburnum

Fragrant snowball viburnum

Korean spice viburnum

Gloriously clothed with color every spring, this mature border of shrubs includes cutleaf Japanese maple, azalea, and pink-flowered dogwood.

Shrubs in nursery containers make an easy transition to the garden.

branches of forsythia, lilac, or viburnum. What a wonderful way to celebrate spring!

■ Plant shrubs that will flower in succession through the growing season. Get some spring, summer, and fall bloomers—then play them up, using other plants as supporting characters. Match the flower color of a viburnum with a cluster of daffodils. Echo the color of an azalea with a pot of pink pansies.

SHRUBS IN CONTAINERS

Any hardy shrub you find growing in a container at the garden center can continue life as a container plant on your terrace, deck, or doorstep. Use a larger container with additional potting soil of the type preferred by the plant. Set the plant and its container in the right amount of sun or shade. In cold climates, use frostproof containers such as redwood or plastic. Avoid terra-cotta, which can crack if the soil freezes. Other factors to keep in mind are the size and density of the shrub and its appearance at different times of the year.

■ Plant a coniferous shrub garden for winter fun. Use evergreens with a variety of different shapes and leaf colors—gold, blue, gray, and green. In northern climates where winter is long, this kind of planting brightens the garden.

Suitable shrubs include dwarf firs, pines, hemlocks, spruces, heathers, junipers, arborvitaes, and false cypresses. Specialty nurseries and catalogs abound with other, less common conifers as well. Interplant cone-shape and vertical evergreens with low and mounded forms. Add some spectacular weeping conifers for excitement, and contrast blue and gray foliage against green and gold. In summer, add some annuals, perennials, and ornamental grasses for variety.

Shrubs and trees lend form and texture to a barren winter landscape.

Once established, woody plants need surprisingly little maintenance to keep them healthy and beautiful.

PLANTING AND CARE

Once planted and established, woody plants need little care—much less than most plants. They do have a few continuing needs, however, including mulching, feeding, watering, pest control, and pruning. Consider the following tips:

■ Slice off circling or tangled roots before planting shrubs grown in containers. Potted shrubs fill the container with roots, which then twine around and around. New roots may continue this destructive pattern even when planted if the old circling roots are not removed. Eventually, the crown may be strangled by its own roots.

Use a pair of sharp pruning shears to slice off circling roots and to loosen up dense, matted roots. Releasing the healthy roots inside the root-ball, planting the shrub in good soil, and keeping the

To ensure good results after planting, don't let the roots go into the soil dehydrated. An hour in a bucket of room-temperature water is all it takes. Plant immediately after soaking, and keep moist through the entire first growing season.

soil moist will encourage vigorous new root growth.

■ Soak the roots of bare-root shrubs before planting. Bare-root shrubs are dug in fall or spring, washed clean of soil, and shipped directly to mail-order catalog customers. Shrubs commonly sold bare-root include Chinese abelia, bloodtwig dogwood, button-bushes, viburnums, some forsythias, winterberry holly, and beauty bush, as well as hedge shrubs such as spirea.

■ Score the sides of the planting hole to encourage root penetration. In clay soils, slick-sided holes can dry to a glaze that is difficult for young roots to penetrate.

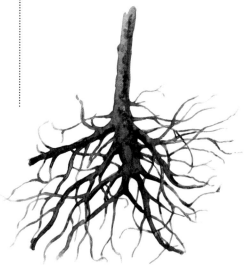

Slicing into the hole perimeter with your shovel breaks up the glazing and creates openings where roots can move out.

■ Thin out a third to a half of the branches of bare-root shrubs before planting. Your pruning shears will become one of your best planting tools, helping you put the shrub into a healthy balance before planting.

When shrubs are dug from the nursery field and processed for shipping, they lose most of their feeding roots, the delicate young roots responsible for absorbing

SOME SHRUBS FOR SEASONAL BLOOMS

Spring

- Azaleas
- Rhododendrons
- Ornamental quince
- Cotoneaster
- Forsythia
- Fothergilla
- Lilac
- Viburnum

Summer

- Butterfly bush
- Scotch heather
- Blue spirea
- Summersweet
- Hydrangea
- Rose-of-Sharon
- Saint-John's-wort
- Potentilla
- Spirea

Fall

- Butterfly bush
- Rose-of-Sharon
- Witch hazel

moisture. Until the shrub is replanted and reestablishes new feeding roots, it can't support all the growth it once did. Pruning reduces shoots to balance root loss.

When pruning, begin by removing old, weak, damaged, or crowded branches at their bases. But don't indiscriminately shear off the top of the plant. The terminal buds on the branch tips release hormones that encourage root growth and maintain a slow, orderly pattern of growth. These are both desirable qualities worth preserving in your shrubs.

■ Deadhead hybrid rhododendrons and mountain laurels to increase next year's bloom. Once the flowers begin to fade, use your thumb and forefinger (or pruning shears) to cut off the soft, immature flowering cluster. Just be careful not to damage nearby buds or shoots, which will soon be sprouting into new branches.

■ Consider changing an overgrown shrub into a multistemmed tree. This works nicely with flowering plums, black haw viburnums, chastetree, and lilacs, all of which can grow to be 12 to 15 feet tall.

A winged euonymus shrub can become a tree.

Begin by removing small, crowded upright stems to reveal a handful of shapely mature branches that can serve as trunks. Remove side shoots from the trunks up to about 5 feet off the ground, creating a tree form. Continue pruning as needed to keep the trunks clear of growth.

■ Wrap boxwood and other broad-leaf evergreen shrubs with burlap to prevent winter burn. When the soil is frozen, the sun is bright, and the wind is strong, evergreens lose moisture from their exposed leaves and cannot replace the moisture through frozen roots. The foliage scorches to brown and the stems may die back—or even worse, the whole shrub may die. Burlap makes a coat for the shrub and ensures that you will have a nice-looking plant waiting for you when spring arrives. This also works for coniferous evergreens like arborvitae. Be sure to water these shrubs well in the fall so they'll have plenty of moisture stored.

■ Build a temporary wire frame around tender shrubs—the species most likely to suffer winter damage in your area— and fill it with straw or leaves for winter protection. Like padding a carton of valuables, this provides insulation from winter's worst cold.

■ Do not plant boxwood and other brittle-stem shrubs near the foundation of your house.

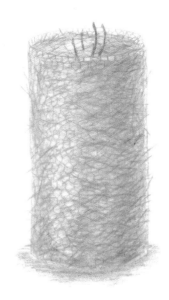

Heavy, wet, melting snow or chunks of ice can slip off the roof and flatten shrubs residing below.

FLOWERING TREES

MAKING YOUR SELECTIONS

Flowering trees can be one of the most memorable elements of the landscape. Fragrant flowering crab apples; frothy, aromatic fringe tree flowers; and weeping cherries dripping with pink blossoms can linger in the mind well after the flowers are gone.

Flowering trees make excellent accents when planted alone; this is a good use for them on small lots. For larger areas, you can mass them or repeat them to define a straight or curved line. Many flowering trees offer all-season interest, with showy spring flowers, green or purple-bronze leaves in summer, vividly colored leaves in fall, and bright fruit or attractive bark in fall or winter.

■ Flowering trees can be an excellent addition to a yard with few perennial flowers. In this case, pay particular attention to tree bark as you make your selections. Tree

Lacy dogwoods thrive at woodland's edge where light is filtered but plentiful.

bark—silver, black, red, or green, either smooth or textured—can be beautiful and adds winter interest to your yard. Consider, for example, stewartia's peeling bark of gray, brown, orange, or red, as well as its creamy summer flowers and great fall color. The paper bark maple, with only small, early spring flowers, has glowing, rust-colored bark and leaves that light up orange and red in fall. Colorful fall fruits provide a feast for the eyes as well as for the birds.

SOME SMALLER FLOWERING TREES

Crab apple

Hawthorn

Yellowwood

Palo verde

Flowering cherry

Flowering plum

Redbud

Dogwood

Mountain ash

Tree lilac

Star magnolia and other
  magnolias

Witch hazel

■ Choose a flowering tree over a shade tree for a small garden. Not only is the size right— you'll also get beautiful flowers as a bonus.

• Trees that stay under 15 feet tall include 'Spring Glory' amelanchier, 'Crusader' hawthorn, fringe tree, and 'Camelot' crab apple. See the list on page 279 for more ideas.

• Trees that stay between 15 and 30 feet include 'Autumn Brilliance' amelanchier, redbuds, and kousa dogwoods.

■ Choose trees that cast light shade if you want to plant a flower garden beneath them. Some trees allow sunlight to filter down between open branches or small leaves. Small, weeping, or long-trunked trees allow light to reach the flowers from the side during the morning and afternoon. Some good choices for mixed flower beds include crab apples, flowering plums, flowering cherries, franklin tree, golden rain tree, and Japanese tree lilac. Among the shade trees, consider honey locusts, ironwood, and birches.

■ Choose trees that have wide crotch angles to avoid weak branches and ice damage. The

This strong tree has wide crotch angles.

on trees like Bradford pears and plums, is that they are not well supported on the trunk. If coated with ice in a winter storm, they may split off. The narrow branching angle can also catch moisture and encourage diseases.

Another problem can arise when upright-growing branches with narrow crotch angles near the top of a young tree begin to grow as fast as the main trunk. Prune the branches back to keep the trunk taller and dominant. If allowed to continue in this way, the tree develops a split leader, two trunks growing side by side. In severe weather, the trunks can crack apart, and the tree may be finished for good.

crotch (or branch) angle measures the distance between the trunk and the base of the branch. An upright branch has a narrow crotch angle of less than 45 degrees. A sturdy, wide-angled branch has a 45- to 60-degree crotch angle.

The problem with branches that have narrow crotch angles, a common occurrence

■ Avoid planting large-fruited trees over patios and decks. Large crab apples, apples, pears, and other fruits and berries can mar the patio and furniture and make steps slippery. Sweet, ripe fruit can attract yellow jackets and other critters. Let large fruits look pretty from afar, where they can drop unheeded in mulch, lawn, or ground cover. For outdoor living areas, choose tree cultivars with

Pollinators like honeybees ensure a beautiful crop of crab apples.

SOME CRAB APPLES WITH SMALL FRUIT

'American Masterpiece'

'American Salute'

'Christmas Holly'

'Donald Wyman'

'Louisa'*

M. sargentii

'Weeping Candied Apple'

'Spring Snow' (no fruit)

'Camelot'*

'Cankerberry'

'Cinderella'*

'Excaliber'*

'Guinevere'*

'Lancelot'*

'Snowdrift'*

*Excellent choices for disease resistance

small or persistent fruit that won't drop and cause a mess.

∎ Buy flowering trees in the spring. Trees purchased in the fall have probably been sitting in the nursery lot all summer.

PLANTING AND CARE

∎ Use spreaders on young fruit trees to correct narrow branch angles. Fruit trees are particularly prone to developing upright branches. Not only do these branches have all the problems mentioned on page 281, but they also grow tall and wild instead of slowing down to flower and fruit. Shifting them into a more productive mode begins with creating a wider branch angle.

When the tree is young and flexible, you can prop short struts in the gap between a shoot and the trunk to force the branch down into a better

45-degree angle. Slightly older branches can be tied to a stake or weight to pull them down into position. Once the branches mature enough to become firm and woody, you can remove the spreaders and the branches will stay in place.

∎ Pull or cut off the burlap before covering the roots with

soil when planting balled and burlapped stock. This simple bit of housekeeping can mean the difference between success and failure for the tree. Some trees are wrapped with synthetic burlap, which will not decay thus preventing the roots from growing free. Even natural-fiber burlap left around the roots can be slow to decay. It can wick moisture away from the young roots, a sure way to cause damage.

■ Carefully consider planting depth before digging the hole for a new tree. You should make the hole twice as wide as the root-ball but no deeper than it. Setting the ball on solid ground that has not been fluffed by tilling or shoveling provides a firm foundation. If the soil underneath settles or shifts, the tree can sit too deep in the ground.

If planting in heavy clay soil, you can plant high so that the top third to top half of the root-ball is above the soil surface. This allows some roots to get out of soggy, poorly aerated soil. Fill in around the exposed roots with good soil, and top with mulch.

■ Check the accuracy of your planting hole depth using a shovel handle. When you think the hole may be deep enough, set the root-ball inside. Lay the shovel handle across the top of the hole. It should be even with or slightly lower than the top of the root-ball.

■ Plant groups of flowering trees in beds. When growing in

Group shrubs and trees for maximum impact and lower maintenance.

Planting ground cover under your trees, rather than adding mulch, has a number of benefits.

• In poor soils, roots can grow freely through the entire amended bed.

• You can water and fertilize the entire group at the same time.

• The problem of mowing or trimming around the trunks is eliminated, saving time and damage to the bark.

• You can plant a shade garden in the grove.

clusters or groves, flowering trees look spectacular in the landscape, much more so than isolated individual trees. There are other advantages to planting larger groupings of trees:

■ Plant ground covers beneath your trees if you don't want a sea of mulch under them. Ground covers become a carpet of greenery and prevent mowing complications and root competition that can plague trees planted in turf.

Shade Trees and Evergreens

Shade trees and evergreens are the largest elements in the landscape, well able to complement even the biggest house. Use them to frame your home, but plan ahead to ensure that the trees will not become overwhelming; if you have a smaller house, you should plant smaller trees than if you have a very large home. With each passing year, big trees grow more valuable, increasing the worth of your house and property.

SELECTING TREES FOR YOUR LANDSCAPE

CLIMATE ZONES AND WOODY PLANTS

Like perennials, trees and other woody plants have multiple factors that affect their hardiness in a particular site. Cold tolerance is a primary determi-nant. You can't grow an orange tree in Minnesota unless you grow it in a greenhouse to protect it from freezing temperatures. Landscape plants tolerate varying degrees of cold, as measured by the USDA Hardiness Zone Map (see pages 312–313). Each plant is assigned to a zone range where it is most likely to succeed. But hardiness zones are only indications.

Mature trees at regular intervals along a road or driveway provide distinction and drama as well as shade.

■ Consider other factors, such as good snow cover, protection from the wind, and excellent growing conditions. You may be able to stretch the zone somewhat if you understand microclimates and use winter mulches. Within a species, certain plants may be hardier than average and are often used to breed hardier varieties.

■ Check with local nurseries and botanical gardens for information concerning cold hardiness as well as whether a given plant will do well under local conditions. Always ask before you buy. A good nursery will sell those plants that are right for the region's climate.

DESIGNING WITH WOODIES

When adding trees to your landscape, it's important to assess their various landscape functions. Consider their size and shape and whether or not they are evergreen or deciduous. Do they offer flowers, fruit, or berries? In what season are they most colorful? Is fruit drop going to be a problem? Do the leaves change color in the fall? The design ideas that follow will help you determine which trees might be the best fit for your landscape needs.

■ Use a medley of shapes to create design interest that goes much deeper than the leaves and flowers. Massing many specimens of the same type of tree can also contribute to a coherent, attractive design.

■ If you already have large trees on your property, the new plantings should blend with them, not be dwarfed by them. It may take larger masses or larger specimens to do the job.

■ Enjoy a tree that can double as a sculpture by planting a

A curly-limbed willow tree makes a unique addition to the landscape.

290 ■ Shade Trees and Evergreens

curly-limbed willow. Twisted branches and curling leaves make interesting focal points on small willows such as 'Golden Curls' and 'Scarlet Curls.'

■ Include some shade trees with bold fall color for an exciting finish to the growing season. As autumn approaches, trees begin breaking down green chlorophyll and storing the components away for winter. This reveals underlying leaf coloration, which was there all along but hidden beneath the green pigments.

A bright burst of color is one of autumn's special delights.

A narrow tree fits nicely into a small garden space or corner.

Among the best trees for fall color are black gum, maple, birch, sourwood, ginkgo, tulip tree, red oak, hickory, and white ash such as 'Autumn Applause,' all of which are outstanding when nights are cool and days are sunny.

■ Add upright accents in narrow spaces (such as courtyard gardens) with special, extra-slender trees. Some examples are 'Columnaris' European hornbeam, 'Dawyck' European beech, 'Princeton Sentry' ginkgo, and 'Columnaris' Swiss stone pine.

■ Add spice to the landscape by growing peacocks, which are trees with uniquely colored foliage held all season long. Some choices you might consider are red-leaved Japanese maples, golden-leaved box elders and catalpas, or purple-leaved beech trees.

Some trees with colorful foliage are commonly available at garden centers and nurseries. Others can be found at specialty nurseries.

SIZE AND GROWTH

Woody plants, unlike herbaceous perennials, retain the previous years' growth and build on it, becoming much larger with time. A tree may take 30 to 100 years to reach its full height.

This European white birch could be replaced by a disease-resistant cultivar of birch.

SLOWER-GROWING TREES

- Red maple
- Sugar maple
- Ginkgo
- Sycamore
- White oak
- Bur oak
- Pin oak
- English oak
- Pines
- Spruces
- Sourwood
- Lindens

■ Choose younger and smaller trees to plant over larger ones. The motto "bigger is better" is not true when it comes to trees. Although you can have nearly full-size trees planted in your yard (at a whopping price), smaller trees transplant more easily and grow more quickly than larger trees. They also cost less and are easier to handle without hiring landscapers.

It's best to start with a tree that has a 1- to 1½-inch trunk diameter (officially called its *caliper*). Very small seedlings—the kind given away by forestry departments on Arbor Day—are a little too diminutive. They take a long time to grow large enough to be noticed in the garden, especially if hidden amid grass.

■ When planting fast-growing trees, start with economical and quick-developing bare-root saplings. Fast-growing trees will increase in height by several feet a year. Under ideal conditions, a young tree that stands 3 feet tall upon planting will be up to 5, 6, or 7 feet tall the next year. The following year, it may be 10 feet tall or larger.

All trees require time to reach their prime, but fast growers stay on the move and hardly test your patience at all.

Make sure the plants you buy are the right size for the job. Tiny seedlings may get lost.

FAST-GROWING TREES

These can fill the yard fast, but they may not be as sturdy and long-lived as slower growers.

- Ash
- Poplars
- Willows
- Arizona cypress
- Eucalyptus
- Catalpa
- Honey locust
- Hackberry
- Red mulberry
- Tulip tree
- Cork tree
- Japanese pagoda tree

Thornless honeylocust is a safe and beautiful street or lawn tree—a vast improvement over its thorny wild relatives.

■ Look to slower-growing trees for long, trouble-free lives and enough strength to withstand wind and ice storms.

■ Plant fast-growing trees with slower-growing species to get shade fast. As the slower-growing trees get large enough to make an impact on the yard, cut out the weaker fast growers. You end up with the best of both worlds— quick greenery and lasting strength. See pages 292–293 for lists of possible trees to plant.

PREVENTING PROBLEMS

■ Choose pest- or disease-resistant species or varieties instead of problem-plagued trees. When you take the time to select a tree ideally suited for your site, your chances of long-term success are great. But they're even better when you check the track record of the tree you have in mind. If it's prone to insect or disease attack, continue your studies to find alternative, untroubled species or varieties. Because large shade trees can live for decades, even centuries, spending an extra hour or two determining the best tree to plant will pay off for a long, long time.

Instead of European white birch, try disease-resistant river, 'Monarch,' or 'Avalanche' birches. A substitute for a weak-wooded silver maple tree is 'Celebration' maple. Try substituting 'Crusader' hawthorn for rust-susceptible hawthorns, and 'Metroshade' plane trees for disease-susceptible London plane trees.

■ Inspect trees for any girdling roots, which can squeeze a tree trunk and cut off its food supply.

Girdling roots are common on container-grown plants. It begins when circling

roots reach upward and loop around the bottom of the trunk. As the trunk grows wider, the roots cut into it and can strangle it. In less severe cases, girdling roots may only cut into one side of the tree, causing death of limbs serviced by the damaged wood.

If you inadvertently buy a tree with girdling roots, use your pruning shears to cut them off where they emerge from the crown before planting.

■ Check trees for deep root collars. The root collar is the junction of roots and trunk, an important place that should be kept level with or above the soil surface when planting.

Sometimes when nurseries cultivate between rows of field-grown trees and shrubs, extra soil gets thrown up above the roots and around the base of the trunk. When the root-ball is dug up and wrapped in burlap, the bottom of the trunk (and the top of the roots) may actually be deep in the ball, with only barren soil above. This leaves the tree shortchanged on roots and the root collar unnaturally deep.

If the nursery will allow, pull back the burlap and brush back the soil to look for the junction of root and trunk.

ESTABLISHING AND MAINTAINING YOUR TREES

PLANTING TIPS

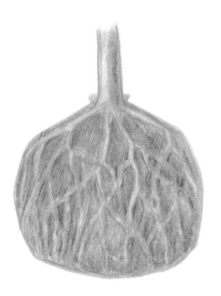

■ Plant trees in a wide, shallow hole, at least twice the width of the root-ball. In the past, gardeners have been advised to plant trees in holes of many different shapes and sizes. But contemporary recommendations reflect new findings in how tree roots grow. Many trees concentrate

■ Skip staking unless you are planting young trees in areas prone to strong winds. Staking can actually do more harm than good for young trees. If staked improperly, with rubbing or tight wires, the bark and trunk can become damaged, sometimes irreparably.

their feeding roots in the top foot of soil. A wide hole loosens up an open, surface-hugging expanse for the early growth of these roots and will help young trees become established more quickly. There is no need to amend the soil—trees thrive best when they are established in native soil.

■ After planting, water well but do not overwater. Continue watering as needed, and do not let the soil dry out completely until the plant is well established, which can take a year or two, even if it is a drought-tolerant species.

If you need to stake a tree, do it gently so the tree can still move.

Staking also interferes with the natural movement of a tree swaying in the wind. Recent research has shown that swaying helps trees develop stronger, tapered trunks that will serve them well and keep them sturdy for decades.

Where staking can't be avoided, use flexible stakes and ties that have a couple inches of slack so the tree can continue to move. Pad the trunk or slip a section of rubber hose over the supporting wire so it won't damage the tree. Remove the stakes as soon as the tree has rooted enough to become self-supporting.

■ Plant evergreens in spring or summer up to about mid-August, but no later. To support their foliage through winter, they need to have a well-established root system and plenty of internal moisture before the ground freezes.

■ Avoid planting trees that deer especially enjoy eating where deer are abundant. Some of their favorites include yews, arborvitaes, junipers, and some pines. Concentrate instead on some of their least favorite trees, including maples, beeches,

Deer prefer certain trees—like yews—so you should plant trees they'll avoid.

ashes, ginkgoes, honey locusts, tulip trees, sour gums, spruces, sycamores, oaks, willows, and bald cypresses.

CARE AND PRUNING

Once planted and established, a woody plant needs little care—much less than most other plants. It has a few continuing needs to attend to, including mulching, feeding, watering, pest control, and pruning.

■ Wrap the trunk of thin-barked trees, most notably fruit trees, in winter to help keep the bark from splitting. Tree wraps and firmer plastic tree guards can also discourage rabbits and rodents from chewing on the bark and can prevent accidental damage from mowers.

Remove the tree wrap in the spring so it won't get too tight on the swelling trunk or provide a hiding place for pests.

■ Adjust how you water a young tree as it gets established. When it is first planted and for the following growing season, provide water directly on the planting site. You can allow a hose to trickle gently over the root-ball, making a shallow saucer of soil below the leafy canopy to keep the water from running off.

Once the tree is established enough for new roots to grow vigorously, use soaker hoses to water just outside the

perimeter of the tree canopy. This will encourage the roots to spread outward, providing a stronger foundation for the tree.

■ Mulch the tree properly. Put a layer of bark mulch, wood chips, or compost from the drip line (below the perimeter of the branch canopy) to 4 inches from the trunk (not too close or problems can arise). Mulching will help eliminate weeds and keep the planting site moist. It also looks good and gives the landscape a polished feel.

Avoid excessively thick layers of mulch, which can limit soil aeration in heavy ground and cause roots to smother. Another problem occurs when thick heaps of mulch break down into rich organic matter. Shallow-rooted trees like maples can grow thick root mats in the mulch (which is not good), and some of those roots may start to girdle (which is even worse!). Shallow roots are also subject to excessive drying in summer.

Prepare your trees for winter weather so they will stay moist and healthy.

begins to brown out and then fail. Look for trees that can withstand salt spray. An example of a salt-susceptible evergreen is white pine. Some alternatives include sycamore maple, Austrian black pine, Japanese black pine, red mulberry, and sour gum.

■ Help prepare evergreen trees for dry winter weather by watering them more in the fall, especially when rainfall has been limited. It's also helpful to spray leaves with an antitranspirant coating, which limits evaporation from the foliage.

■ Don't plant salt-susceptible evergreens near the street in cold climates. Salt used for snow and ice control will splash up on the needles and drip into the soil. It won't be long before a thriving tree

■ Prevent summer spider mite attacks on your evergreens by spraying susceptible plants with a hose every day during hot, dry weather. If you're out watering the garden, turn the hose on the evergreen foliage as well. Water helps dislodge spider mites and discourage their multiplication, a great nontoxic preventative.

GARDENING JOURNAL

Date: _____

Weather conditions: _____

_____

What's blooming now? _____

_____

_____

Care and maintenance tasks: _____

_____

_____

Date: _____

Weather conditions: _____

_____

What's blooming now? _____

_____

_____

Care and maintenance tasks: _____

_____

_____

Date: _____

Weather conditions: _____

_____

What's blooming now? _____

_____

_____

Care and maintenance tasks: _____

_____

_____

Date: _____

Weather conditions: _____

_____

What's blooming now? _____

_____

_____

Care and maintenance tasks: _____

_____

_____

Date: _____

Weather conditions: _____

_____

What's blooming now? _____

_____

_____

Care and maintenance tasks: _____

_____

_____

Date: _____

Weather conditions: _____

_____

What's blooming now? _____

_____

_____

Care and maintenance tasks: _____

_____

_____

Date: _____

Weather conditions: _____

_____

What's blooming now? _____

_____

_____

Care and maintenance tasks: _____

_____

_____

Date: _____

Weather conditions: _____

_____

What's blooming now? _____

_____

_____

Care and maintenance tasks: _____

_____

_____

Date: _____

Weather conditions: _____

_____

What's blooming now? _____

_____

_____

Care and maintenance tasks: _____

_____

_____

Date: _____

Weather conditions: _____

_____

What's blooming now? _____

_____

_____

Care and maintenance tasks: _____

_____

_____

Date: _____

Weather conditions: _____

_____

What's blooming now? _____

_____

_____

Care and maintenance tasks: _____

_____

_____

Date: _____

Weather conditions: _____

_____

What's blooming now? _____

_____

_____

Care and maintenance tasks: _____

_____

_____

Date: _____

Weather conditions: _____

_____

What's blooming now? _____

_____

_____

Care and maintenance tasks: _____

_____

_____

Date: _____

Weather conditions: _____

_____

What's blooming now? _____

_____

_____

Care and maintenance tasks: _____

_____

_____

Date: _____

Weather conditions: _____

_____

What's blooming now? _____

_____

_____

Care and maintenance tasks: _____

_____

_____

Date: _____

Weather conditions: _____

_____

What's blooming now? _____

_____

_____

Care and maintenance tasks: _____

_____

_____

Date: _____

Weather conditions: _____

_____

What's blooming now? _____

_____

_____

Care and maintenance tasks: _____

_____

_____

Date: _____

Weather conditions: _____

_____

What's blooming now? _____

_____

_____

Care and maintenance tasks: _____

_____

_____

Date: _____

Weather conditions: _____

_____

What's blooming now? _____

_____

_____

Care and maintenance tasks: _____

_____

_____

Date: _____

Weather conditions: _____

_____

What's blooming now? _____

_____

_____

Care and maintenance tasks: _____

_____

_____

USDA PLANT HARDINESS ZONE MAP

The United States Department of Agriculture Plant Hardiness Zone Map divides North America into 11 zones based on average minimum winter temperatures, with Zone 1 being the coldest and Zone 11 the warmest. Each zone is further divided into sections that represent five-degree differences within each ten-degree zone.

This map should only be used as a general guideline, since the lines of separation between zones are not as clear-cut as they appear. Plants recommended for one zone might do well in the southern part

of the adjoining colder zone, as well as in neighboring warmer zones. Factors such as altitude, exposure to wind, proximity to a large body of water, and amount of available sunlight also contribute to a plant's winter hardiness. Because snow cover insulates plants, winters with little or no snow tend to be more damaging to marginally hardy varieties. Also note that the indicated temperatures are average minimums—some winters will be colder and others warmer.

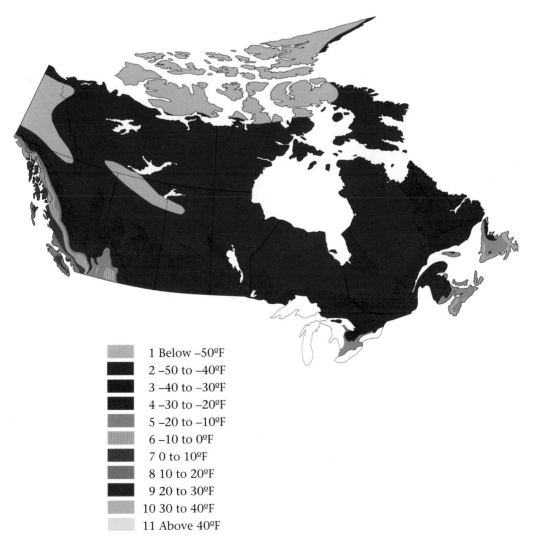

1 Below −50ºF
2 −50 to −40ºF
3 −40 to −30ºF
4 −30 to −20ºF
5 −20 to −10ºF
6 −10 to 0ºF
7 0 to 10ºF
8 10 to 20ºF
9 20 to 30ºF
10 30 to 40ºF
11 Above 40ºF